30-Day
Shadow Work for Millennials

Practical Guide to Healing Hidden Patterns, Perfectionism, Career Burnout, and Social Media Anxiety While Thriving in Modern Life

Wilson Emmanuel Brown

Table of Contents

Preface

This 30-day guide offers a practical, accessible approach to shadow work that addresses the specific challenges your generation faces. You'll explore how social media affects your sense of self, how economic pressures shape your relationship with success, how modern dating creates unique relationship shadows, and how family programming might conflict with your authentic values. Each day provides concrete exercises, reflection questions, and integration practices that help you recognize unconscious patterns and develop more conscious ways of living.

The goal isn't to eliminate problematic aspects of yourself or to become a perfect person. Shadow work is about integration—learning to work consciously with all aspects of your personality so you can choose how to express them rather than being controlled by unconscious patterns. When you integrate your shadow, you gain access to energy, creativity, and authenticity that have been locked away. You become more yourself, not someone else's version of who you should be.

This work isn't always comfortable. You'll discover things about yourself that might initially feel challenging or surprising. You'll need to question assumptions about who you are and what you want that you might have held for years. But on the other side of this discomfort lies a kind of freedom that most people never experience—the freedom to be completely yourself while still maintaining loving relationships and meaningful work.

The format of this book is designed for busy lives and realistic schedules. Each day requires only 15-20 minutes of focused attention, though you may find yourself drawn into deeper reflection on days when the material particularly resonates. The exercises are practical and can be adapted to your specific circumstances. You don't need any previous experience with psychology or personal development work to benefit from this process.

The millennial generation faces unique pressures and opportunities. You're dealing with economic uncertainty, climate anxiety, and social media comparison while also having access to unprecedented information, global connection, and awareness of personal growth possibilities. This combination creates both challenges and potential that shadow work is uniquely positioned to address.

Over the next 30 days, you'll develop skills for recognizing unconscious patterns, communicating more authentically, making decisions from self-awareness rather than external pressure, and creating a life that reflects your genuine values and interests. You'll learn to use creativity for psychological integration, to set boundaries from wholeness rather than defensiveness, and to approach relationships as opportunities for mutual growth rather than performance venues.

By the end of this journey, you won't have eliminated all your problems or achieved perfect self-awareness. But you will have developed a different relationship with yourself—one based on curiosity rather than judgment, integration rather than suppression, and authentic expression rather than managed image. You'll have tools for continuing this work throughout your life as you encounter new situations and continue growing.

This book is an invitation to meet yourself completely and to discover what becomes possible when you stop fighting against parts of yourself and start working with your whole personality consciously. It's an invitation to move beyond the exhausting work of being who you think you should be and into the energizing work of becoming who you actually are.

Introduction: Why Millennials Need Shadow Work

You probably didn't set out to become an expert in managing anxiety, but here you are. You can navigate a panic attack while leading a Zoom meeting, craft the perfect response to a passive-aggressive text, and maintain your Instagram aesthetic while your actual life feels chaotic. These are survival skills nobody taught you explicitly—you developed them because you needed them.

But what about the parts of yourself you had to hide or shut down to develop these capabilities? What happened to your anger when expressing it wasn't safe? Where did your natural creativity go when it became "impractical"? How did you learn to anticipate everyone else's needs while ignoring your own?

This is shadow work territory. Your shadow isn't your dark side or your evil twin. It's simply the parts of yourself that you learned weren't acceptable, safe, or valuable in the world you were growing up in. For millennials, that world was uniquely challenging to navigate authentically.

The Millennial Psychological Landscape

You came of age during a perfect storm of social, economic, and technological changes. The internet arrived when your personalities were still forming, creating the first generation to experience both the connection and isolation of digital life. You watched the adults around you lose jobs, homes, and retirement savings during the 2008 recession, learning early that traditional paths weren't guaranteed. Climate change became undeniable during your formative years, adding existential weight to everyday decisions.

Meanwhile, you were raised by parents who often meant well but were operating from completely different assumptions about how the world worked. Many grew up believing that hard work guaranteed success, that institutions were trustworthy, and that progress was linear. You inherited their advice while living in a reality where none of those assumptions held true.

This created a psychological double bind. You absorbed messages about who you should be while living in conditions that made being that person nearly impossible. The result? Parts of yourself went underground.

The social media Shadow

Consider what happened to your sense of self when Facebook launched during your college years. Suddenly, every moment became potentially public. You learned to curate not just your posts but your experiences, always aware that someone might be watching, judging, comparing.

The person you became online wasn't exactly false, but it wasn't complete either. You emphasized certain traits—the successful, happy, adventurous ones—while de-emphasizing others. Your anger, fear, confusion, and messiness didn't fit the platform, so those parts learned to hide.

This wasn't conscious manipulation. It was adaptation. But adaptation always comes with costs. The parts of yourself that didn't make it into your social media presence didn't disappear—they just became shadows, operating below your conscious awareness.

You might notice this shadow in how you feel after scrolling Instagram—that strange combination of inspiration and inadequacy. Or in how you craft posts, spending more time on the caption than you spent having the experience. These aren't character flaws; they're natural responses to growing up under unprecedented social surveillance.

4

Economic Anxiety and Identity

Your generation entered adulthood during economic uncertainty that your parents' generation didn't face at the same life stage. You were told to follow your passion while watching people with graduate degrees work multiple gig jobs. You learned to hustle while being criticized for lacking loyalty. You adapted to economic instability by becoming incredibly resourceful, but often at the cost of your authentic desires.

Many millennials developed what psychologists call "economic anxiety shadows"—parts of themselves that learned to equate safety with productivity, self-worth with earning potential, and rest with laziness. You became experts at optimizing your life for efficiency and output, sometimes forgetting what you actually wanted underneath all that optimization.

This shows up in interesting ways. You might feel guilty during downtime or judge yourself for not monetizing your hobbies. You might struggle to make decisions without considering their impact on your resume or LinkedIn profile. These aren't personality defects— they're psychological adaptations to economic pressure that previous generations didn't face at your age.

The Climate Anxiety Shadow

You're the first generation to grow up knowing that the planet's stability isn't guaranteed. This awareness shaped your psyche in ways that are just beginning to be understood. While previous generations could assume a predictable future, you learned to live with existential uncertainty as background noise.

This created what researchers call "climate anxiety"—not just worry about environmental issues, but a deep psychological impact from knowing that many adult promises about how life works might not hold true for your lifetime. The shadow side of this awareness often shows up as nihilism, perfectionism, or a sense that nothing you do matters.

You might notice this shadow in your relationship to planning. Some millennials become hyper-planners, trying to control an uncertain future through detailed preparation. Others swing the opposite direction, struggling to plan at all because the future feels too uncertain. Both responses make perfect sense given the conditions you grew up in.

The Relationship Shadow

Dating apps arrived just as you were learning how to form adult relationships. This timing wasn't accidental—it fundamentally shaped how your generation approaches intimacy. You learned to present yourselves as products, to handle rejection as data, and to maintain multiple connections simultaneously.

These skills served you in some ways. You became comfortable with ambiguity, good at reading subtle social cues, and capable of maintaining connections across distances. But you also learned to suppress certain needs that didn't fit dating app culture.

Your need for consistency, depth, and emotional safety had to adapt to a culture of infinite options and casual communication. Parts of you that craved commitment learned to appear "chill." Parts that needed emotional security learned to seem low-maintenance. These adaptations weren't wrong, but they created shadows—authentic needs that learned to hide.

The Family Pattern Shadow

Your parents often meant well, but they raised you for a world that no longer existed by the time you reached adulthood. They taught you strategies that worked in their context but created internal conflict in yours. You learned to achieve in school systems that no longer predicted career success. You absorbed work ethics designed for jobs that no longer existed. You inherited financial advice that assumed economic conditions that had already changed.

This created a psychological split between your inherited programming and your lived experience. The parts of you that wanted

6

to follow family values often conflicted with the parts that needed to adapt to current reality. Rather than resolving this conflict consciously, many millennials simply compartmentalized— following family expectations in some areas while secretly adapting in others.

You might notice this shadow in how you talk to your parents about your life. There might be subjects you avoid or ways you edit your experiences to match their expectations. This isn't dishonesty—it's an attempt to maintain connection while living authentically. But it requires keeping parts of yourself in the shadows.

Why Shadow Work Now

You've spent your twenties and early thirties adapting to conditions nobody prepared you for. You developed incredible resilience, creativity, and resourcefulness. But adaptation always requires compromise, and some of those compromises are ready to be revisited.

Shadow work isn't about judging the choices you made or the parts of yourself you had to hide. It's about recognizing that you have more options now. The survival strategies that got you through your twenties might not be serving your thirties. The parts of yourself you had to suppress might be ready to contribute to your life in new ways.

This work is particularly important for millennials because you're entering your peak influence years. You're becoming the managers, parents, and leaders who will shape the next generation's experience. The unconscious patterns you carry will inevitably affect the people around you. Shadow work helps ensure that you're passing on your wisdom rather than your wounds.

What This Guide Offers

Over the next thirty days, you'll develop a different relationship with the parts of yourself you've been avoiding. You'll learn to recognize when your shadows are running the show and how to work with them consciously. You'll discover that many of your "problems" are actually solutions that outlived their usefulness.

This isn't therapy, though it might complement therapeutic work you're doing. It's not a cure for mental health conditions, though it might help you understand your patterns more clearly. It's simply a structured way to develop awareness of unconscious patterns and make more conscious choices about which parts of yourself you want leading your life.

You won't become a different person. You'll become more yourself—including the parts you've been keeping in the shadows. This integration doesn't solve all problems, but it often makes problems more workable because you're addressing them with your full capacity rather than just the parts of yourself you consider acceptable.

With this foundation established, we're ready to begin the actual work of recognition, understanding, and integration that will unfold over the next thirty days.

How to Use This Guide

You're holding something different from the typical self-help book. This isn't meant to sit on your shelf looking impressive—it's designed to be marked up, written in, and carried with you through thirty days of real change.

Think of this guide as your personal laboratory for understanding the parts of yourself you've been avoiding. Every millennial carries invisible baggage from growing up in a world that changed faster than anyone could adapt to. Social media arrived when we were forming our identities. The economy crashed when we were supposed to be launching careers. Climate change became undeniable when we were planning our futures. This guide helps you work with the psychological residue from all of that.

The 30-Day Structure

Each day offers exactly what you need without overwhelming your already-packed schedule. You'll spend about 15-20 minutes with the material, though some days might pull you in deeper. That's perfectly normal.

Daily Format:

- **Check-In** (2-3 minutes): A simple way to ground yourself before diving in

- **Core Teaching** (5-8 minutes reading): One focused concept with examples you'll recognize

- **Exercise** (8-12 minutes): Hands-on work that reveals patterns and possibilities

- **Integration** (2-5 minutes): How to carry the day's insight into your actual life

The first week focuses on recognition—spotting the shadows that have been running parts of your life without your permission. Week two gets more specific about where these patterns came from and how they show up now. Week three is about integration—befriending these parts of yourself rather than fighting them. The final week helps you live from this new awareness.

What You'll Need

A pen or pencil, obviously. Some people prefer writing by hand for this kind of work because it engages different parts of your brain. Others find typing easier. Use whatever helps you be honest with yourself.

You'll also need patience with the process. Shadow work isn't about quick fixes or motivational highs. It's about developing a different relationship with the parts of yourself you've been taught to hide or fix. Some days will feel like breakthroughs. Other days will feel messy or confusing. Both are exactly right.

Working with Resistance

Your mind will find creative ways to avoid this work. It might tell you this is self-indulgent or that you don't have time. It might make you suddenly remember urgent tasks right when you sit down with the guide. This resistance isn't a character flaw—it's your psyche protecting patterns that once served you.

When resistance shows up, acknowledge it: "There's the part of me that thinks this is silly" or "Here's the voice saying I should be more productive." Then gently return to the day's work. You're not trying to eliminate resistance, just not letting it run the show.

Privacy and Safety

This work is for you alone unless you choose to share it. Some exercises might bring up memories or emotions you haven't felt in a while. That's normal, but if you find yourself overwhelmed or if traumatic memories surface, consider reaching out to a therapist who understands this kind of inner work.

You're not trying to process everything at once. You're simply developing awareness of patterns that have been unconscious. There's a difference between exploring your shadows and drowning in them.

When Life Gets in the Way

Some days you won't have twenty minutes. Some days you'll be dealing with crises or simply forget. This doesn't mean you've failed or need to start over. Just return to wherever you left off.

The guide is designed to work with real life, not perfect conditions. If you miss a few days, notice what pulled you away. Sometimes avoidance is part of the pattern worth examining. Other times, life genuinely requires your attention elsewhere. You'll know the difference.

Getting the Most from This Experience

Be curious rather than judgmental about what you discover. The goal isn't to become a different person—it's to become more honest about who you already are. Your shadows aren't enemies to defeat; they're parts of yourself that developed for good reasons and might need new jobs now.

Write in the margins. Skip exercises that don't resonate. Add extra thoughts to ones that do. This is your guide, not a test you need to pass perfectly.

Some insights will hit immediately. Others will make sense weeks or months later. Trust that something is working even when you can't see it yet. Shadow work often happens in layers, with deeper understanding emerging over time.

The people around you might notice changes before you do. You might find yourself less reactive in certain situations, more willing to speak up in others, or simply more comfortable in your own skin. These shifts often happen gradually, like adjusting to a new prescription for glasses—suddenly you realize you've been seeing more clearly.

Day 1: Meeting Your Millennial Shadow Self

Daily Check-In

Before we start, take a moment to notice how you're feeling right now. Are you curious? Skeptical? A little anxious about what you might discover? Whatever's present is perfectly fine. You're about to meet parts of yourself that have been working behind the scenes for years, and it's natural to feel uncertain about that process.

You've probably noticed times when you react more strongly to situations than seems warranted, or when you find yourself doing things that don't align with who you think you are. Maybe you're usually calm but lose it completely when someone interrupts you. Perhaps you consider yourself confident but become paralyzed when it's time to negotiate salary. These moments point to your shadow—the parts of your personality that operate outside your conscious awareness.

Understanding Your Shadow

Your shadow isn't your evil side or your inner demon. It's simply the collection of traits, emotions, and impulses that you learned weren't safe, acceptable, or valuable to express. Every person develops a shadow because growing up requires adapting to the people and circumstances around you.

Think about it this way: imagine you're naturally a pretty direct person, but you grew up in a family where direct communication was seen as rude or aggressive. You'd learn to suppress that directness to maintain connection and approval. That directness doesn't disappear—it just goes underground, becoming part of your shadow.

Later in life, it might show up as passive-aggression, sudden outbursts when you're overwhelmed, or a deep discomfort around conflict.

For your generation, this process happened during particularly intense social conditions. You developed your sense of self while navigating unprecedented changes in technology, economics, and social expectations. The parts of yourself that didn't fit those rapidly changing conditions had to adapt quickly or go into hiding.

The Millennial Shadow Formation

Your shadow formed differently than previous generations' shadows because the world you grew up in was uniquely unstable. Your parents' generation could develop their identities assuming that the future would look roughly like the present. You couldn't make that assumption.

This created what psychologists call "adaptive shadows"— personality traits that went underground not because they were inherently problematic, but because they didn't match the conditions you were trying to navigate. Your natural rebelliousness might have become hidden when you needed to be the "good kid" during your parents' divorce. Your tendency to dream big might have gone into hiding when the economy crashed and practicality became survival.

The result is that many millennials carry shadows that aren't about bad impulses, but about good impulses that learned they weren't welcome. Your shadow might contain your natural leadership abilities, your artistic talents, your capacity for rest, or your ability to set firm boundaries. These aren't character defects—they're strengths that went underground when circumstances demanded different qualities.

How Shadows Operate

Your shadow influences your life whether you're aware of it or not. It shows up in several predictable ways:

Projection: You might find yourself intensely annoyed by traits in other people that you actually possess but don't acknowledge in yourself. If you've suppressed your own neediness, you might be particularly irritated by people who seem demanding or high-maintenance.

Compensation: Sometimes you develop the opposite trait to an extreme degree to balance what's in your shadow. If you've hidden your vulnerability, you might become hyper-independent, refusing help even when it would benefit you.

Sudden Emergence: Your shadow traits might burst through during stress, illness, or major life changes. The person who's usually incredibly organized might become chaotic during a breakup. The perpetually optimistic person might become unexpectedly cynical when facing a career setback.

One person described their shadow emergence this way: "I always prided myself on being low-maintenance and easy-going. Then I moved in with a romantic partner and suddenly I had opinions about everything—how to load the dishwasher, which direction the toilet paper should hang, when to leave for appointments. I didn't recognize myself."

This isn't a breakdown—it's actually your psyche trying to restore balance by bringing hidden parts of yourself back into consciousness.

The Millennial Context

Your generation faced particular challenges that shaped your shadows in specific ways. You learned to navigate social media during your formative years, which meant developing a public self that was optimized for approval and engagement. The parts of you that were messy, uncertain, or still developing had to learn to hide.

You also came of age during economic instability, which meant that practical considerations often overruled personal preferences. Many millennials have shadows that contain their authentic desires—the careers they actually wanted, the lifestyles they preferred, the values they held before survival became the priority.

Additionally, you were raised during the height of the self-esteem movement, which paradoxically created shadows around anything that felt like weakness or failure. You learned to present yourselves as confident and capable, sometimes hiding the parts that needed help, felt lost, or struggled with basic adult tasks.

Setting Up Your Practice Space

Shadow work requires both courage and safety. You're going to be looking at parts of yourself that you've been avoiding, and that process works best when you feel secure enough to be honest.

Physical Space: Choose a place where you won't be interrupted or feel self-conscious. This might be your bedroom, a coffee shop where nobody knows you, or even your car during lunch break. The key is privacy and comfort.

Emotional Safety: You're not trying to change anything yet—just notice what's there. Think of yourself as a curious scientist observing your own patterns rather than a judge evaluating your character.

Pace Control: You get to decide how deep to go each day. If something feels overwhelming, you can slow down or take a break. This isn't a race or a test you need to pass.

Support: While this work is private, it can be helpful to have someone you trust available if you need to talk through what comes up. This might be a friend, therapist, or family member who understands you're doing some self-reflection work.

Exercise: First Shadow Glimpse

This exercise helps you begin recognizing how your shadow operates in daily life. You'll look for patterns that might point to hidden aspects of your personality.

Step 1: Identify Your Irritations

Think about the last week and recall three people or situations that bothered you more than they probably should have. Write them down along with what specifically irritated you.

For example:

- Coworker who constantly needs reassurance about their work

- Friend who posts too many vacation photos on Instagram

- Neighbor who plays music too loud late at night

Step 2: Look for the Pattern

For each irritation, ask yourself: *What trait or behavior am I reacting to so strongly?*

Then ask: *Is there any way I might have this same trait, even in a different form?*

The coworker's need for reassurance might trigger you because you've learned to hide your own insecurity. The vacation photos might bother you because you've suppressed your own desire to be seen and celebrated. The loud music might irritate you because you've learned to always consider others' needs before your own.

Step 3: Explore Without Judgment

Pick one of these patterns and spend a few minutes writing about it. Don't try to fix anything or judge yourself. Just get curious.

When did I learn that this trait wasn't okay to have?

What would happen if I allowed myself to express this quality in healthy ways?

How might my life be different if I didn't have to hide this part of myself?

Step 4: Notice Your Resistance

Pay attention to any part of you that wants to dismiss this exercise or argue with your discoveries. That resistance is also valuable information—it's often your psyche's way of protecting you from seeing something you're not ready to integrate yet.

Write down any resistance you notice: "Part of me thinks this is ridiculous because..." or "I'm having trouble believing that I could be..."

This resistance isn't a problem—it's just another piece of data about how your shadow operates.

Reflection Questions

What surprised you about this exercise?

Which of your irritations felt most charged or emotional?

What do you notice about the parts of yourself you work hardest to hide?

How do you think your shadow traits might actually be strengths in disguise?

Daily Integration

For the rest of today, practice noticing your reactions to other people without trying to change them. When someone annoys you, gets under your skin, or triggers a strong response, just get curious: *What might this be showing me about myself?*

You don't need to analyze every reaction or turn every interaction into a therapy session. Just develop the habit of asking the question. Sometimes the answer will be clear, sometimes it won't. Both outcomes are useful.

Remember that this work isn't about becoming a different person—it's about becoming more aware of who you already are. Your shadow contains both challenges and gifts, and learning to work with it consciously gives you access to more of your full capacity.

Tomorrow's Preparation

Tonight, pay attention to your social media usage. Don't change anything yet—just notice how you feel before, during, and after scrolling through various platforms. We'll use these observations as raw material for tomorrow's exploration of how social media interactions reveal shadow patterns.

You're not broken and don't need fixing. You're simply beginning to see the full spectrum of who you are.

Having mapped this initial terrain, we're ready to explore how your shadow shows up in the digital spaces that have become central to millennial life and identity formation.

Day 2: The social media Mirror: Instagram Envy & TikTok Triggers

Daily Check-In

Before opening any apps, take a moment to check in with yourself. How are you feeling right now—before you see anyone else's curated highlights? Notice your energy level, mood, and any expectations you have about what you might see online today.

You've probably experienced that strange feeling of scrolling through social media and ending up in a worse mood than when you started, even when you saw mostly positive content from people you care about. Or maybe you've caught yourself crafting the perfect caption for longer than you actually spent having the experience you're posting about. These moments reveal something important about how social media interacts with the hidden parts of your personality.

Social media platforms didn't create your shadow, but they've become powerful tools for revealing it. Every post, like, and comment involves unconscious choices about which parts of yourself to show and which to hide. Over time, these micro-decisions shape both your online presence and your offline self-perception in ways you might not realize.

How social media Reveals Your Shadow

When you scroll through Instagram or TikTok, you're not just consuming content—you're engaging in a complex psychological process of comparison, projection, and identity negotiation. Your reactions to other people's posts often say more about your hidden dynamics than about the content itself.

Consider what happens when you see someone posting about their new job, relationship milestone, or vacation. If you feel genuinely happy for them, that's usually your authentic self responding. But if you feel a twist of envy, inadequacy, or the urge to mentally critique their post, you're probably encountering your shadow.

That envy isn't necessarily about wanting their specific job or vacation. It's often about wanting permission to celebrate yourself the way they're celebrating themselves, or wanting the confidence to share your wins without worrying about others' reactions. The critique might be your mind's way of protecting you from feeling inferior by finding ways to dismiss their success.

One person noticed this pattern: "I realized I was always finding something wrong with people's engagement photos—the ring was too flashy, the location was too generic, the caption was too sappy. Then I got engaged and was terrified to post about it because I was so worried about being judged the same way I'd been judging others."

The Millennial social media Shadow

Your generation had the unique experience of developing your identity both online and offline simultaneously. You learned to navigate real-world social dynamics while also managing your digital presence, often without clear guidance about how to do either well.

This created several common shadow patterns:

The Performance Shadow: Parts of you that learned to optimize for likes, comments, and engagement rather than authentic expression. You might find yourself experiencing life through the lens of "how will this look online?" or feeling disappointed when real experiences don't match their social media potential.

The Comparison Shadow: The parts of you that use other people's highlight reels to judge your bchind-thc-sccnes reality. This shadow convinces you that everyone else has figured out adulting, relationships, or career success while you're still struggling with basics.

The Authentication Shadow: The aspects of yourself that feel too messy, uncertain, or human for public consumption. This shadow keeps your real struggles, doubts, and imperfections carefully hidden while presenting a polished version of your life.

The Engagement Shadow: Parts of you that learned to measure your worth through social media metrics. You might check your phone compulsively after posting, feel deflated when content doesn't perform well, or find yourself crafting posts designed to generate specific responses rather than express authentic thoughts.

The Instagram Envy Pattern

Instagram envy reveals some of the most common millennial shadows. When you feel that familiar pang while looking at someone's seemingly perfect life, you're usually encountering parts of yourself that feel inadequate or unfulfilled.

But here's what's interesting: you're rarely envious of things you genuinely don't want. The person posting gym selfies probably isn't triggering envy in someone who truly loves their sedentary lifestyle. The travel blogger isn't making someone who prefers staying home feel inadequate. Envy usually points to desires you've been suppressing or goals you've convinced yourself aren't realistic.

A recent graduate described this realization: "I kept getting annoyed at people posting about their new apartments, their weekend plans, their seemingly perfect relationships. I told myself I didn't care about that stuff, that I was focused on more important things. But the intensity of my reaction showed me that I did want those things—I just didn't believe I could have them or deserve them."

The shadow here isn't the desire itself, but the belief that you can't or shouldn't pursue what you actually want. Social media becomes a daily reminder of the gap between your authentic desires and what you're allowing yourself to pursue.

TikTok Triggers and Identity

TikTok operates differently than Instagram but reveals shadow patterns just as clearly. The algorithm serves you content based on your engagement patterns, creating a feedback loop that can illuminate both your conscious interests and your unconscious preoccupations.

Pay attention to the content that makes you feel uncomfortable, defensive, or triggered. Someone talking about setting boundaries might irritate you if you've suppressed your own need for boundaries. Financial advice content might trigger shame if you've been avoiding dealing with money issues. Relationship content might bring up feelings about your own romantic situation that you haven't fully acknowledged.

The "For You" page essentially becomes a mirror showing you what you're drawn to and what you're avoiding. Your shadow often reveals itself in the gap between what you think you should be interested in and what actually captures your attention.

Exercise: Digital Shadow Mapping

This exercise helps you identify specific ways your shadow shows up in your social media experience.

Step 1: The Envy Audit

Think about the last few times you felt envious, irritated, or triggered by someone's social media post. Write down:

- What the post was about

- Your specific emotional reaction

- What story you told yourself about their post or their life

- What you wished you could have or do instead

Step 2: The Posting Pattern Analysis

Look at your last 10-15 posts across all platforms. For each one, ask yourself:

What was I hoping people would think or feel when they saw this?

What parts of this experience did I not share, and why?

How did I feel before and after posting this?

If I'm honest, was I seeking any specific type of response?

Step 3: The Algorithm Mirror

Spend 10 minutes scrolling through TikTok or Instagram without engaging (no likes, comments, or saves). Just observe what content appears and notice your internal reactions. Write down:

- Which posts made you feel good about yourself
- Which posts made you feel worse about yourself
- What patterns you notice in the content the algorithm shows you
- Any themes that seem to repeatedly appear

Step 4: The Curation Check

Look at your own profile as if you were seeing it for the first time. Ask yourself:

What impression would someone get about my life from my posts?

What aspects of my actual life are missing from this representation?

What would I post if I weren't concerned about others' reactions?

How much energy do I spend managing my online image?

Reflection Questions

Which social media platform triggers the most comparison or envy for you, and why might that be?

What aspects of your personality show up online versus the parts that stay private?

How has your relationship with social media changed as you've gotten older?

What would it feel like to post something without checking to see how it performed?

Creating Healthy Social Media Boundaries

Understanding your social media shadows is the first step toward using these platforms more consciously. This doesn't mean you need to quit social media or dramatically change your online behavior. It means becoming aware of the unconscious patterns so you can make more intentional choices.

Time Boundaries: Notice when you use social media to avoid feelings or responsibilities. Set specific times for checking apps rather than scrolling mindlessly throughout the day.

Content Boundaries: Unfollow or mute accounts that consistently trigger comparison or negative self-talk. You can appreciate someone's success without subjecting yourself to daily reminders of what you feel you lack.

Emotional Boundaries: Before posting, ask yourself what you're hoping to get from sharing this content. If you're seeking validation for your worth as a person, that's usually your shadow talking.

Reality Boundaries: Remember that social media shows you curated moments, not complete lives. Everyone struggles with things they don't post about.

Daily Integration

Today, practice what one person called "shadow-aware scrolling." Before opening any social media app, set an intention to notice your emotional reactions without judging them. When you feel envy, comparison, or irritation, get curious about what those feelings might be showing you about your own desires or insecurities.

You don't need to analyze every post or turn social media into a therapy session. Just develop awareness of how these platforms interact with your shadow patterns. Sometimes this awareness alone is enough to shift your relationship with social media in healthier directions.

Remember that recognizing these patterns isn't about judging yourself for having them. Everyone who uses social media navigates these dynamics. The difference is whether you're doing it consciously or unconsciously.

Tomorrow's Preparation

As you go through your workday, pay attention to moments when you feel stressed, overwhelmed, or inadequate. Notice any stories you tell yourself about your career progress, professional worth, or future prospects. We'll use these observations to explore how your shadow shows up in workplace dynamics and career decisions.

Now that you've explored this territory, you have a clearer sense of how your hidden patterns influence your digital life, creating space to examine how similar dynamics play out in your professional world.

Day 3: Workplace Burnout and Career Shadow Patterns

Daily Check-In

Before diving into work today (or before reflecting on work if you're doing this exercise outside of business hours), pause and notice how you feel when you think about your career. Is there excitement? Anxiety? A sense of being behind or not measuring up? Whatever comes up, let it be there without trying to fix it right away.

You probably didn't expect career anxiety to be this persistent. Maybe you thought that once you got a good job, or finished your degree, or reached a certain salary, the underlying stress would ease up. Instead, many millennials find that workplace anxiety just shifts forms—from worrying about getting hired to worrying about getting promoted, from imposter syndrome to burnout, from job insecurity to the pressure of having too many options.

These career shadows often develop because your generation entered the workforce during a period of massive economic and technological change. The career advice you received growing up doesn't match the reality you're living in, creating internal conflicts between what you think you should want professionally and what actually makes sense in your current circumstances.

The Millennial Career Shadow Formation

Your relationship with work developed during a unique historical moment. You were told to follow your passion while watching people with graduate degrees struggle to find stable employment. You learned about the importance of work-life balance while witnessing older colleagues work themselves to exhaustion just to maintain middle-class lifestyles.

This created what psychologists call "aspirational shadows"—parts of your professional identity that went underground because they didn't match economic reality. Your shadow might contain your idealistic career goals, your need for creative fulfillment, your desire for work-life balance, or your expectation that hard work should lead to financial security.

Conversely, your shadow might also contain qualities that don't fit the modern workplace but that you actually need: your natural competitiveness, your desire for recognition, your need for structure and hierarchy, or your preference for deep focus over constant collaboration.

One person described it this way: "I always thought I was just being practical by choosing the safe career path, but I realized I'd completely buried my entrepreneurial side. I used to have tons of business ideas and creative projects, but somewhere along the way I decided those were unrealistic daydreams. Now I feel resentful about my stable job because it's not feeding the part of me that wants to build something."

Common Millennial Workplace Shadows

The Achievement Shadow: This shows up as either compulsive overwork or complete avoidance of professional goals. You might find yourself unable to relax because there's always more you could be doing to advance your career. Or you might procrastinate on important projects because the pressure to excel feels overwhelming.

The Security Shadow: Parts of you that prioritize stability over satisfaction, sometimes to an extreme degree. You might stay in jobs that drain you because they offer good benefits, or you might avoid career risks that could lead to greater fulfillment because they threaten your financial security.

The Authenticity Shadow: Aspects of your personality that don't fit professional norms get suppressed. Your humor might be too irreverent, your communication style too direct, or your interests too niche for your workplace culture. Over time, you learn to hide these parts so completely that you forget they exist.

The Ambition Shadow: This can go two directions. Either you've suppressed your natural ambition because it doesn't feel safe or socially acceptable, leading to underachievement and resentment. Or you've developed excessive ambition to compensate for feeling powerless in other areas of life.

Imposter Syndrome as Shadow Projection

Imposter syndrome is one of the most common ways career shadows manifest for millennials. You feel like you're faking competence and that eventually someone will discover you don't belong in your role. But imposter syndrome isn't really about your qualifications—it's about the gap between who you think you should be professionally and who you actually are.

The "imposter" feeling often points to authentic parts of yourself that don't match your professional identity. Maybe you're naturally collaborative but work in a competitive environment. Maybe you're a big-picture thinker but your job requires attention to detail. Maybe you value creativity but work in a highly structured field.

Instead of recognizing these as natural mismatches that could be addressed, your mind creates a story that you're inadequate or fraudulent. The real issue isn't that you lack competence—it's that you're trying to succeed by hiding significant aspects of your personality.

A marketing professional realized this about their imposter syndrome: "I kept feeling like I wasn't strategic enough, wasn't analytical enough, wasn't business-minded enough. But when I looked at my actual track record, my projects succeeded because I brought intuition and emotional intelligence to the work. I was judging myself for not being someone else instead of appreciating what I actually contributed."

The Burnout-Shadow Connection

Millennial workplace burnout often has shadow dynamics underneath it. When you're constantly trying to prove yourself while suppressing parts of your authentic personality, work becomes exhausting on levels beyond the actual tasks you're completing.

Burnout frequently happens when you're working hard to maintain a professional identity that requires hiding too much of who you actually are. The energy it takes to suppress your natural communication style, your genuine interests, your need for creative expression, or your personal values adds invisible weight to every workday.

Additionally, many millennials developed "productive shadows"— parts of themselves that learned to equate worth with output. If you grew up hearing that hard work guarantees success, parts of you might believe that any struggle means you're not working hard enough. This leads to working longer hours when you actually need to work more strategically.

Exercise: Career Shadow Analysis

This exercise helps you identify the hidden patterns affecting your professional life and career satisfaction.

Step 1: The Professional Persona Audit

Write a job description for yourself as if you were hiring someone to play your professional role. Include not just your official duties, but the personality traits, communication style, and values that seem required for success in your position.

Then write a description of your authentic personality, communication style, and values outside of work.

Where do these two descriptions align?

Where do they conflict?

What parts of your authentic self don't show up at work?

Step 2: The Career Story Analysis

Write about your career journey so far, including:

- What you thought you wanted when you were starting out
- What you actually pursued and why
- Times when you felt most and least satisfied at work
- Career decisions you made that you still feel conflicted about
- Professional goals you've given up on or stopped talking about

What patterns do you notice in when you felt energized versus drained?

Which career decisions were made from fear versus excitement?

What professional dreams did you abandon, and why?

Step 3: The Workplace Trigger Inventory

Think about the last few months at work and identify situations that triggered strong emotional reactions. Write down:

- Meetings or interactions that left you feeling frustrated or inadequate
- Colleagues whose behavior bothers you more than it probably should
- Work tasks that you procrastinate on or avoid
- Professional situations that make you feel especially competitive or defensive

What themes do you notice in these triggers?

How might these reactions point to parts of yourself you've suppressed?

Step 4: The Energy Assessment

For each major aspect of your current job (meetings, individual work, client interactions, administrative tasks, creative projects, etc.), rate your energy level from 1-5:

1 = Completely drains me
2 = Usually tiring
3 = Neutral
4 = Usually energizing
5 = Completely energizes me

What patterns do you notice in what energizes versus drains you?

How might these energy patterns reflect authentic aspects of your personality?

What would happen if you structured more of your work around your natural energy patterns?

Reflection Questions

What aspects of your authentic personality feel unwelcome in your workplace?

How has your relationship with ambition changed since entering the workforce?

What would you pursue professionally if you weren't worried about others' opinions or financial security?

When do you feel most like yourself at work versus when do you feel like you're performing a role?

Healthy Ambition and Shadow-Driven Overwork

Learning to work with your career shadows doesn't mean lowering your professional standards or avoiding challenging goals. It means distinguishing between ambition that comes from your authentic interests and values versus ambition driven by unconscious needs to prove yourself or compensate for feelings of inadequacy.

Healthy Ambition usually feels energizing, aligns with your natural interests, and allows for flexibility in how goals are achieved. You can enjoy the process as well as anticipate the outcome. You're motivated by genuine excitement about what you might create or contribute.

Shadow-Driven Overwork often feels compulsive and is accompanied by anxiety about not doing enough. The goals themselves matter less than what achieving them might prove about your worth. You focus exclusively on outcomes and feel anxious whenever you're not actively working toward your goals.

One way to test this: imagine achieving your professional goal and then no one noticing or congratulating you. If that scenario devastates you, your motivation might have shadow elements. If you'd still feel satisfied because the work itself was meaningful, you're probably operating from healthy ambition.

Daily Integration

Today, practice noticing the difference between tasks that energize you and tasks that drain you, without trying to change anything yet. Pay attention to moments when you feel most like yourself at work versus when you feel like you're performing a role.

Also notice your internal dialogue during challenging work situations. Are you encouraging yourself the way you'd encourage a good friend, or are you more critical? The voice of harsh self-judgment often carries shadow material—parts of yourself that learned that your natural pace, style, or approach wasn't acceptable.

Remember that recognizing these patterns is different from judging yourself for having them. Everyone navigates career decisions with incomplete information while trying to balance competing needs and values. The goal isn't to have made perfect choices, but to make more conscious choices going forward.

Tomorrow's Preparation

As you move through today, notice your relationship with money—not just how much you have or spend, but how you feel about money in general. Pay attention to any anxiety, shame, or stories you tell yourself about your financial situation or money management skills. These observations will help us explore how your shadow affects your relationship with financial security and decision-making.

With these tools in your toolkit, you're ready to examine how similar shadow dynamics influence your relationship with money and financial decision-making, an area where millennial experience often differs significantly from previous generations.

Day 4: Financial Anxiety and Student Debt Shadows

Daily Check-In

Before looking at your bank account, checking your credit card balance, or thinking about any bills you need to pay, pause and notice how you feel in your body right now. What happens when you imagine dealing with financial tasks today? Do you feel tension anywhere? Avoidance? A sense of dread or inadequacy?

Money carries emotional weight for everyone, but millennials often carry particularly complex financial shadows. You came of age during economic instability, were encouraged to invest in education that led to unprecedented student debt levels, and entered a job market where traditional financial milestones became much harder to achieve. The result is that many millennials have complicated relationships with money that go far beyond their actual financial circumstances.

Your money shadows aren't just about the numbers in your accounts. They're about the stories you tell yourself about what those numbers mean about your worth, your competence, and your future possibilities. These stories often operate below conscious awareness, influencing financial decisions in ways that can sabotage your long-term security and happiness.

The Millennial Financial Shadow Formation

Your generation received financial advice based on economic conditions that no longer existed by the time you needed to apply it. You were told that college debt was "good debt" that would lead to higher earnings, that homeownership was a key milestone of adult success, and that consistent saving and investing would ensure comfortable retirement.

Meanwhile, you've lived through multiple economic disruptions, watched housing costs outpace income growth, and witnessed people with advanced degrees struggle to find stable employment. This created a psychological split between inherited financial beliefs and lived financial reality.

Many millennials developed what economists call "financial trauma shadows"—unconscious patterns that formed as protective responses to economic uncertainty. Your shadow might contain your natural optimism about the future, your ability to take calculated financial risks, your sense of deserving financial security, or your capacity to enjoy money when you have it.

Conversely, your shadow might also contain unrealistic financial expectations, entitled attitudes about lifestyle, or avoidance patterns that prevent you from dealing with money issues constructively. The key is that these patterns operate unconsciously, making financial decisions more emotionally charged than they need to be.

Common Financial Shadow Patterns

The Scarcity Shadow: This shows up as chronic anxiety about never having enough money, even when your basic needs are met. You might hoard money instead of spending it on things that would improve your life, or constantly worry about financial catastrophes that are statistically unlikely to occur.

The Avoidance Shadow: Parts of you that learned to cope with financial stress by not thinking about money at all. You might procrastinate on budgeting, avoid checking account balances, or make financial decisions impulsively to avoid the anxiety of planning carefully.

The Shame Shadow: Beliefs that your financial situation reflects your personal worth or competence. This shadow convinces you that people who are financially successful are inherently better, smarter, or more disciplined than people who struggle with money.

The Comparison Shadow: Using other people's apparent financial success to judge your own situation. You might feel inadequate when friends buy houses, go on expensive vacations, or seem to have more disposable income, even when you don't know the complete picture of their financial circumstances.

The Rebellion Shadow: Unconscious resistance to financial planning or conventional money advice, sometimes because it feels like giving up on dreams or accepting limitations you don't want to accept. This might show up as overspending on experiences or avoiding practical financial steps.

Student Debt and Identity

For many millennials, student loan debt created a specific type of financial shadow. You were told that education was an investment in your future, but many discovered that the debt felt more like punishment than investment. This can create internal conflict between the part of you that values education and personal growth and the part that resents the financial burden.

Student debt shadows often show up as:

- Regret about educational choices, even when the education itself was valuable

- Resentment toward people who didn't need to take on debt for their education

- Feeling trapped in jobs or career paths because you need the income to service debt

- Shame about not being able to achieve traditional financial milestones on the expected timeline

- Cynicism about advice to invest in yourself or take career risks

One person described their student debt shadow this way: "I used to be someone who believed that investing in yourself always pays off. But after years of loan payments, I became really risk-averse about spending money on anything that wasn't a guaranteed return. I stopped taking classes, going to conferences, or buying books because I associated learning with debt. I had to consciously separate the value of education from the burden of student loans."

Financial Anxiety and Control

Millennial financial anxiety often has less to do with actual money management skills and more to do with feeling powerless in economic systems that seem rigged against your generation. When traditional financial advice doesn't work in current economic conditions, it's easy to conclude that you're doing something wrong personally rather than recognizing that the systems themselves have changed.

This can create shadow patterns around control and responsibility. You might take excessive personal responsibility for financial challenges that have systemic causes, leading to shame and self-blame. Or you might avoid taking any personal responsibility, feeling that individual financial planning is pointless given economic realities.

The healthy middle ground involves recognizing both systemic economic challenges and your personal agency within those constraints. You can acknowledge that your generation faces unique financial challenges while still taking practical steps to improve your situation within current conditions.

Exercise: Money Story Excavation

This exercise helps you identify the unconscious beliefs and patterns that influence your financial decisions and emotional relationship with money.

Step 1: Your Money Origin Story

Write about your earliest memories related to money. Include:

- How your family talked about money (or didn't talk about it)

- Messages you received about spending, saving, and financial success

- Any significant financial events from your childhood or adolescence

- The first time you remember feeling anxious, ashamed, or excited about money

What patterns do you notice between these early experiences and your current financial attitudes?

Step 2: The Financial Trigger Assessment

Think about recent situations involving money that triggered strong emotional reactions. Write about:

- Times when you felt anxious, angry, or ashamed about financial topics

- People whose financial situations trigger comparison or judgment in you

- Financial decisions you keep putting off or avoiding

- Money conversations that consistently cause conflict in your relationships

What themes emerge in these triggers?

How might these reactions point to beliefs about money that you haven't examined?

Step 3: The Financial Fantasy Exercise

Imagine you suddenly had enough money to cover all your basic needs indefinitely, without having to work for it. Write about:

- How you would spend your time

- What you would do with excess money beyond covering expenses

- How your relationships might change

- What you would worry about if money wasn't a concern

What does this fantasy reveal about what money represents to you beyond purchasing power?

Which aspects of this fantasy could you pursue now in smaller ways?

Step 4: The Money Shadow Dialogue

Write a conversation between two parts of yourself: the part that wants to be responsible with money and the part that resists financial planning. Let each part explain its perspective without judgment.

Responsible part: "We need to budget and save because..."

Resistant part: "But that feels restrictive because..."

Continue this dialogue for several exchanges, letting each part respond authentically.

What does each part want that the other part doesn't understand?

How might both parts' concerns be valid?

Reflection Questions

How has your relationship with money changed since graduating from college or starting your career?

What financial advice have you received that doesn't seem to apply to your actual circumstances?

When do you feel most confident about money versus when do you feel most anxious or inadequate?

What would change about your financial behavior if you fully believed you deserved financial security?

Creating New Financial Narratives

Working with your financial shadows doesn't require completely changing your money management approach, but it does mean becoming conscious of the stories you tell yourself about money and examining whether those stories serve you.

From Scarcity to Sufficiency: Instead of focusing on what you don't have, practice noticing what you do have. This doesn't mean being satisfied with inadequate income, but it means not letting financial anxiety consume emotional energy that could be used more productively.

From Shame to Reality: Your financial situation is data, not a judgment about your character. People's financial circumstances result from a complex mix of personal choices, systemic factors, timing, and luck. You can take responsibility for your financial decisions without taking on shame about your worth as a person.

From Avoidance to Engagement: You don't have to love dealing with money to handle it responsibly. You can acknowledge that financial planning feels boring or overwhelming while still doing it because it serves your long-term interests.

From Comparison to Strategy: Other people's financial situations don't determine what's possible for you. Focus on your own circumstances, values, and goals rather than trying to match what others appear to have achieved.

Daily Integration

Today, practice paying attention to your internal dialogue when money topics come up. Notice whether you encourage yourself or criticize yourself when dealing with financial tasks. Notice whether you approach money decisions from anxiety or from a more neutral, strategic mindset.

Also pay attention to how you feel in your body when thinking about money. Financial anxiety often shows up as physical tension, shallow breathing, or restlessness. These physical cues can help you recognize when your money shadows are activated, creating opportunities to respond more consciously.

Remember that developing a healthier relationship with money is a process, not a destination. Most people have some financial shadows because money represents security, freedom, and status in addition to its practical purchasing power. The goal isn't to eliminate all financial anxiety, but to work with it more skillfully.

Tomorrow's Preparation

As you interact with friends, family, or romantic prospects today, notice your patterns around relationships. Pay attention to how you present yourself, what you hope people will think of you, and what kinds of people you're drawn to or avoid. These observations will help us explore how your shadow influences your relationship choices and romantic patterns.

From this place of knowing, you're ready to examine how similar unconscious patterns influence your relationships and romantic life, areas where shadow projections often play out most dramatically.

Day 5: Dating App Culture and Relationship Projections

Daily Check-In

Before thinking about your romantic life or relationship status, take a moment to notice how you feel about yourself right now, independent of anyone else's opinion. What's your internal sense of your own worth and desirability? How does that change when you imagine being evaluated by someone you're attracted to?

Dating as a millennial means navigating relationship dynamics that no previous generation experienced. You're forming romantic connections through apps that gamify attraction, trying to build intimacy in a culture of infinite options, and learning relationship skills while carrying economic and social stresses that affect partnership possibilities. These conditions create unique relationship shadows that influence not just who you date, but how you see yourself in romantic contexts.

Your relationship shadows aren't just about your dating behavior. They're about the parts of yourself that you've learned to hide or amplify when seeking romantic connection, and the unconscious patterns that influence who you're attracted to and why. These shadows often reveal themselves most clearly in the gap between what you say you want in relationships and what you actually choose.

How Dating Apps Reveal Your Shadow

Dating apps create a unique psychological environment where you must present yourself as a product while simultaneously evaluating others as potential purchases. This dynamic activates several shadow patterns that might not be as obvious in organic relationship formation.

The Marketing Shadow: You learn to highlight your most attractive qualities while downplaying anything that might reduce your appeal. Over time, you might lose touch with which aspects of your personality are authentic versus which ones are optimized for dating success.

The Shopping Shadow: The abundance of options can activate unconscious beliefs that there's always someone better available, making it difficult to appreciate the people you actually meet. You might find yourself comparing every date to an imaginary perfect person who combines the best qualities of everyone you've ever been attracted to.

The Rejection Shadow: The efficiency of app-based rejection can trigger deep insecurities about your fundamental desirability. You might develop protective strategies like being less vulnerable, more entertaining, or more physically available than feels natural to you.

One person described their dating app shadow realization: "I noticed I was becoming someone I didn't recognize on dates. I was funnier, more agreeable, and more sexually available than I actually am, because I was so afraid of being rejected. Then I'd feel disappointed when guys seemed interested in this performance version of me, because I knew it wasn't sustainable."

Millennial Relationship Shadow Formation

Your generation learned about relationships during a period of rapidly changing social norms around gender roles, sexual behavior, commitment timelines, and lifestyle expectations. Many of the relationship models you inherited from family don't match current dating realities, creating internal conflicts about what you want versus what seems possible or acceptable.

The Commitment Shadow: Parts of you that desire deep partnership might conflict with parts that value independence, career flexibility, or personal growth. You might find yourself attracted to unavailable people because they don't trigger your fear of losing autonomy, or avoiding available people because they make commitment feel too real.

The Vulnerability Shadow: Modern dating often requires sharing personal information quickly while maintaining emotional protection against disappointment. You might develop patterns of being simultaneously too open and too guarded, sharing intimate details about your life while keeping your genuine needs and feelings hidden.

The Authenticity Shadow: The pressure to be your best self on every date can create exhaustion around romantic interactions. Parts of your authentic personality—your need for alone time, your processing style, your emotional patterns—might go underground because they don't fit dating culture expectations.

Shadow Projections in Attraction

You're often most attracted to people who embody qualities that exist in your shadow. If you've suppressed your own confidence, you might be drawn to very self-assured people. If you've hidden your emotional intensity, you might find yourself attracted to dramatic partners. If you've learned to be overly responsible, you might be drawn to people who seem carefree and spontaneous.

These attractions aren't necessarily problematic, but they become complicated when you expect your partner to provide qualities that you've disowned in yourself. The confident person might not actually be as secure as they appear. The dramatic person might be exhausting to live with daily. The carefree person might be irresponsible about important matters.

Additionally, you might find yourself consistently annoyed by certain types of people in dating contexts. The person who's too eager might trigger judgments if you've suppressed your own enthusiasm. The person who's too picky might irritate you if you've hidden your own high standards. These reactions often point to shadow projections rather than genuine incompatibilities.

The Anxious-Avoidant Shadow Dance

Many millennials find themselves in relationship patterns where they're either anxiously pursuing connection or avoidantly protecting independence, sometimes switching between these styles with the same person. This often reflects shadow dynamics where parts of your authentic attachment needs are in conflict.

The Anxious Shadow: Parts of you that need reassurance and consistency might show up as clingy or demanding behavior when you're worried about losing someone. You might find yourself checking their social media obsessively, reading too much into response times, or seeking constant validation about the relationship status.

The Avoidant Shadow: Parts of you that need autonomy and space might show up as emotional distancing when relationships start feeling too serious. You might find yourself becoming critical of partners when they want more commitment, or losing interest when someone becomes too available.

The shadow element is that both strategies usually contain valid needs that haven't been integrated consciously. The anxious behavior might mask a genuine need for security and consistency. The avoidant behavior might mask a genuine need for respect and independence. Problems arise when these needs get expressed through unconscious patterns rather than direct communication.

Exercise: Relationship Mirror Work

This exercise helps you identify how your shadow shows up in romantic relationships and influences your attraction patterns.

Step 1: The Attraction Pattern Analysis

Think about the last few people you felt strongly attracted to, whether you dated them or not. For each person, write down:

- What initially attracted you to them

- What you imagined a relationship with them would be like

- What you hoped they would provide in your life

- Any ways they reminded you of family members or past partners

What patterns do you notice in who you're drawn to?

Which of these attractive qualities do you possess but might not express fully?

Step 2: The Dating Persona Assessment

Compare how you present yourself in dating contexts versus how you are with close friends or family. Write about:

- Aspects of your personality that you emphasize when dating

- Parts of yourself that you downplay or hide during early relationship stages

- How your communication style changes in romantic versus platonic contexts

- What you worry potential partners will think about your authentic personality

What does this comparison reveal about which parts of yourself feel safe to share romantically?

Step 3: The Relationship Trigger Inventory

Think about behaviors from past or current romantic partners that triggered strong reactions in you. Write about:

- Partner behaviors that made you feel particularly annoyed, disappointed, or frustrated

- Relationship situations that brought out jealousy, insecurity, or anger in you

- Times when you found yourself being critical or judgmental of a partner's choices

- Moments when you felt like you needed to change or fix someone you were dating

How might these triggers relate to parts of yourself you've suppressed or rejected?

What patterns do you notice in what bothers you about romantic partners?

Step 4: The Relationship Fantasy Exploration

Describe your ideal romantic relationship in detail, including:

- How you and your partner would communicate

- What your daily life together would look like

- How you would handle conflicts and disagreements

- What role the relationship would play in your overall life

Then ask yourself:

Which aspects of this fantasy require changes from your partner versus changes in yourself?

What prevents you from embodying the partner qualities you want to receive?

How might this fantasy reflect parts of yourself you want to develop?

Reflection Questions

How has your approach to dating changed since you started using apps or online platforms?

What relationship advice have you received that doesn't match your actual dating experiences?

When do you feel most like yourself in romantic contexts versus when do you feel like you're performing?

What would change about your relationship patterns if you fully accepted all aspects of your personality as loveable?

Breaking Cycles of Unavailable Partner Attraction

Many millennials find themselves repeatedly attracted to partners who aren't emotionally available, geographically accessible, or genuinely interested in commitment. This pattern often reflects shadow dynamics where parts of yourself aren't available for the kind of relationship you say you want.

If you're consistently drawn to unavailable partners, consider:

- Whether you're actually available for the commitment level you think you want

- What emotional work you might be avoiding by focusing on partners who can't fully show up

- Whether your lifestyle, priorities, or emotional patterns support the relationship you say you desire

- What you might be afraid of about being in a truly available, mutual partnership

The goal isn't to judge yourself for these patterns, but to bring them into consciousness so you can make more intentional choices. Sometimes the issue is that you need to develop more availability within yourself before you can recognize and appreciate availability in others.

Daily Integration

Today, practice noticing the difference between authentic attraction and shadow projection in your interactions with others. When you feel drawn to someone or irritated by someone, get curious about what that reaction might reveal about parts of yourself.

Also pay attention to how you present yourself in any social contexts that might have romantic potential. Notice when you're being genuine versus when you're managing your image. Neither approach is wrong, but awareness gives you more choices about how to engage.

Remember that everyone has relationship shadows, and recognizing yours doesn't mean judging your past choices or current patterns. It means becoming more conscious about what you're actually seeking in romantic relationships and why.

Tomorrow's Preparation

As you interact with family members today (whether in person, via phone, or just thinking about them), pay attention to how your personality shifts in family contexts. Notice which aspects of yourself feel welcomed by your family versus which parts you've learned to hide or modify around them. These observations will help us explore how family shadows affect your adult identity and decision-making.

As this understanding settles, you're ready to explore how similar shadow dynamics play out in family relationships, where many of our deepest patterns first formed and continue to influence our choices as adults.

Day 6: Family Programming vs. Your Millennial Values

Daily Check-In

Before thinking about your family relationships, take a moment to notice how you feel when you imagine having an honest conversation with your parents about your actual life choices, values, and struggles. Does that thought bring up comfort, anxiety, or something in between? Whatever comes up is information about how your family dynamics have shaped your sense of self.

You probably love your family and appreciate many things they taught you, while also recognizing that some of their advice doesn't apply to your current reality. Maybe they encouraged you to stay loyal to employers who don't show loyalty back, or they worry about career moves that actually make sense given today's economic conditions. These disconnects aren't anyone's fault, but they can create internal conflicts between honoring your family's values and living authentically in your own circumstances.

The generational gap between millennials and their parents isn't just about technology or cultural preferences. It's about fundamentally different assumptions about how the world works, what strategies lead to success, and what constitutes a meaningful life. These differences can create family shadows—parts of yourself that you hide or modify to maintain family harmony, even when doing so conflicts with your authentic needs and values.

Generational Value Conflicts

Your parents likely grew up in economic conditions where certain strategies reliably led to security and success. Work hard at one company and they'll take care of you. Buy a house as soon as possible because real estate always appreciates. Get a college degree to ensure stable employment. Save consistently and you'll retire comfortably.

Many of these strategies worked for their generation but don't work the same way for yours. Company loyalty rarely leads to job security anymore. Housing costs have outpaced income growth in most areas. College degrees don't guarantee stable employment. Traditional retirement planning assumes economic stability that many millennials haven't experienced.

This creates what psychologists call "intergenerational dissonance"— internal conflict between inherited family programming and current life requirements. Your family's advice comes from genuine care and their own successful experiences, but applying it literally might actually harm your prospects in today's conditions.

The shadow element emerges when you feel like you have to choose between disappointing your family and living authentically. Parts of your personality, values, or life choices might go underground to avoid family conflict or judgment, even when those parts represent healthy adaptation to current circumstances.

Millennial Family Shadows

The Independence Shadow: Your parents might equate needing help with failure, based on their experience of achieving milestones independently. But millennials often need family financial support, career networking, or emotional support longer than previous generations. You might feel shame about needing help that's actually reasonable given current conditions.

The Stability Shadow: Family pressure to prioritize security over satisfaction might conflict with your need to take calculated risks for career growth or personal fulfillment. You might hide your entrepreneurial interests, creative pursuits, or unconventional career moves because they don't match family definitions of success.

The Relationship Shadow: Your family's expectations about dating, marriage, and family formation timelines might not match current social and economic realities. You might feel pressured to settle down before you're ready or judged for prioritizing personal growth over traditional relationship milestones.

The Lifestyle Shadow: Generational differences in spending priorities, living arrangements, or life experiences might create judgment or misunderstanding. Your parents might not understand why you spend money on experiences instead of saving for a house, or why you value work-life balance over maximizing income.

The People-Pleasing Family Pattern

Many millennials developed strong people-pleasing patterns within their families, especially if their parents were dealing with economic stress, divorce, or other challenges during their formative years. You might have learned to be the "good kid" who didn't add to family stress by having needs or causing problems.

These patterns can continue into adulthood, where you edit your life choices to avoid disappointing your family, even when those choices would serve your best interests. You might choose careers, partners, or life paths based more on family approval than personal authenticity.

One person recognized this pattern: "I realized I was making major life decisions based on what would make my parents proud rather than what would make me happy. I stayed in a corporate job I hated because they could understand and respect it, while I kept my artistic interests secret. I was living their version of success while feeling empty inside."

This isn't about rejecting your family's values entirely. It's about distinguishing between values that still serve you and programming that might need updating for your circumstances.

Breaking Free from Inherited Patterns

Working with family shadows doesn't mean rejecting your family or dismissing their influence. It means becoming conscious about which family patterns serve your current life and which ones might need modification.

Inherited Strengths: Your family likely gave you valuable qualities like work ethic, resilience, loyalty, or problem-solving skills. These strengths can be honored while adapting their expression to current conditions.

Outdated Strategies: Some family strategies that worked in their context might need updating for yours. This doesn't make the strategies wrong, just contextually inappropriate.

Hidden Conflicts: You might have internalized family conflicts that aren't actually your own. For example, if your parents had unresolved issues about money, creativity, or success, you might carry those conflicts unconsciously.

Unexpressed Parts: Aspects of your personality that didn't fit your family's dynamics might have gone into hiding. These could include your natural leadership style, emotional intensity, intellectual curiosity, or artistic sensibilities.

Exercise: Family Pattern Analysis

This exercise helps you identify specific ways that family programming influences your adult choices and which patterns might benefit from conscious examination.

Step 1: The Family Values Audit

Write down the core values your family emphasized while you were growing up. Include both explicitly stated values and values that were demonstrated through behavior. Consider areas like:

- Work and career success
- Money and financial security
- Relationships and family formation
- Personal expression and creativity

- Risk-taking versus safety

- Individual achievement versus family loyalty

- Emotional expression and vulnerability

Which of these values still feel authentic and useful to you?

Which feel outdated or problematic given your current circumstances?

Which values do you find yourself defending even when they don't serve you?

Step 2: The Family Role Assessment

Think about the role you played in your family growing up and how that role continues to influence your adult behavior. Consider:

- Were you the responsible one, the creative one, the problem-solver, the peacemaker?

- What did your family need from you that you provided?

- What aspects of your personality were encouraged versus discouraged?

- How do you still play this role in family interactions?

How does this family role show up in your current relationships and career choices?

What parts of your authentic personality didn't fit your family role?

How might expanding beyond this role serve you now?

Step 3: The Success Definition Comparison

Write two definitions of success: one that reflects your family's values and one that reflects your authentic preferences. Be specific about:

- Career achievements and financial goals

- Relationship and family milestones

- Lifestyle choices and personal fulfillment

- How success is measured and demonstrated

Where do these definitions align and where do they conflict?

Which definition feels more energizing and authentic to you?

What would change in your life if you fully pursued your authentic definition of success?

Step 4: The Family Secret Inventory

Think about aspects of your current life that you don't share fully with your family or that you present differently when talking to them. Consider:

- Career struggles or unconventional choices

- Relationship patterns or dating experiences

- Financial situations or spending priorities

- Personal struggles or mental health challenges

- Lifestyle choices or value differences

What do these secrets reveal about parts of yourself you feel aren't acceptable to your family?

How much energy do you spend managing your family's perception of your life?

What would happen if you were more honest about these aspects of yourself?

Reflection Questions

In what ways do you still seek your family's approval for adult decisions?

What aspects of your personality feel unwelcome in family contexts?

How has your relationship with your family changed as you've become more independent?

What would change about your life choices if you fully trusted that you could maintain family love while living authentically?

Redefining Success Authentically

Creating your own definition of success doesn't mean rejecting everything your family taught you, but it does mean consciously choosing which values to carry forward and which to modify for your circumstances.

From External to Internal Validation: Success becomes about alignment between your choices and your values rather than meeting other people's expectations, even people you love.

From Comparison to Personal Growth: Success becomes about your own development and contribution rather than achieving specific milestones by certain ages.

From Security to Fulfillment: Success includes both practical security and personal satisfaction rather than prioritizing one at the expense of the other.

From Individual to Holistic: Success encompasses your relationships, health, creativity, and community contribution, not just career and financial achievements.

This redefinition process often happens gradually. You might start by making small choices that prioritize your authentic values, then build confidence to make larger decisions from this foundation.

Navigating Family Conversations

As you become clearer about your own values and life direction, you might need to navigate conversations with family members who don't understand or approve of your choices. This doesn't require cutting off relationships, but it does require developing boundaries around which topics are open for family input.

Information Boundaries: You get to decide what information to share and what to keep private. You can love your family while not needing their approval for every life decision.

Advice Boundaries: You can listen to family advice without feeling obligated to follow it. You can appreciate their concern while trusting your own judgment about what works in your circumstances.

Timeline Boundaries: You can acknowledge family concerns about your timeline for various life milestones while making decisions based on your actual readiness and circumstances rather than external pressure.

Value Boundaries: You can respect your family's values while living according to your own. You don't have to convince them that your approach is right, just maintain confidence that it's right for you.

Daily Integration

Today, practice noticing when you modify your behavior, opinions, or self-presentation based on anticipated family reactions. This might happen during phone calls with relatives, when making life decisions, or even when talking to friends about your family.

Pay attention to areas where you feel defensive about your choices. Often, defensiveness points to places where you haven't fully committed to your own path or where you're still seeking approval that might not be available.

Remember that loving your family and living authentically aren't mutually exclusive. Most families can adapt to members growing and changing, especially when those changes are communicated with respect and confidence rather than defensiveness or rebellion.

Tomorrow's Preparation

Tonight, gather your notes from the past six days. We'll be synthesizing your discoveries to create a comprehensive map of your personal shadow patterns. This integration will help you see the connections between different aspects of your shadow and prepare you for the deeper work ahead.

This framework gives us leverage to step back and see the complete picture of how your shadow operates across different life domains, creating a foundation for the integration work that begins next week.

Day 7: Week 1 Integration: Creating Your Shadow Map

Daily Check-In

Take a few moments to acknowledge what you've accomplished this week. You've looked at parts of yourself that most people spend their whole lives avoiding. You've recognized patterns that have been operating unconsciously for years. You've begun the process of bringing hidden aspects of your personality into conscious awareness. That takes courage, and you should feel proud of the work you've done.

As you prepare to create your personal shadow map, notice any resistance that comes up. Your mind might want to minimize what you've discovered, dismiss it as overthinking, or convince you that you don't really need to change anything. This resistance is natural—it's your psyche's way of protecting patterns that once served you, even if they're not serving you now.

Creating a shadow map isn't about fixing yourself or eliminating unwanted traits. It's about developing a clear picture of your complete personality so you can work with all parts of yourself consciously rather than being controlled by patterns you don't recognize.

Your Week's Discoveries

Over the past six days, you've explored how your shadow shows up in different areas of life. Each domain revealed specific patterns, but there are likely threads connecting all these areas that point to deeper themes in your personality structure.

Your social media shadows might connect to your workplace shadows through shared themes about performance and authenticity. Your financial shadows might relate to your relationship shadows

59

through common patterns around worth and security. Your family shadows might underlie all other areas, representing the foundational programming that shaped how you navigate the world.

These connections matter because shadow work isn't about addressing isolated behaviors—it's about understanding the underlying dynamics that create those behaviors across multiple life contexts. When you can see these deeper patterns, you can address root causes rather than just managing symptoms.

Common Themes in Millennial Shadows

As you review your week's discoveries, you might notice some themes that are particularly common for your generation:

Performance versus Authenticity: Growing up with social media, economic pressure, and competitive educational environments often creates tension between presenting a successful image and expressing genuine personality. This theme might show up across work, relationships, and family dynamics.

Security versus Growth: Economic instability and changing career landscapes create ongoing tension between prioritizing safety and pursuing development. This theme might manifest in career decisions, financial choices, and relationship patterns.

Individual Achievement versus Connection: Messages about self-reliance and personal success might conflict with natural needs for community and support. This theme could appear in work dynamics, romantic relationships, and family interactions.

Control versus Acceptance: Facing unprecedented global challenges while receiving advice based on more predictable historical conditions can create excessive focus on controlling outcomes versus accepting uncertainty. This might show up in anxiety patterns, perfectionism, or avoidance behaviors.

One person recognized their overarching theme: "Every area of my life seemed to have the same pattern—I was working incredibly hard to prove that I was worthy of good things instead of just believing I deserved them. At work, in relationships, with money, even on social media, I was constantly trying to earn love and security instead of starting from a place of inherent worth."

Exercise: Personal Shadow Mapping

This exercise helps you synthesize your week's discoveries into a coherent understanding of your personal shadow patterns and their interconnections.

Step 1: Pattern Identification

Review your notes from Days 1-6 and look for repeating themes, similar emotional reactions, or parallel behaviors across different life areas. Write down:

- Emotions that came up repeatedly (shame, anxiety, anger, envy, etc.)

- Behaviors you noticed across multiple contexts (people-pleasing, avoidance, over-achieving, comparison, etc.)

- Internal conflicts that appeared in different forms (authenticity vs. acceptance, security vs. growth, individual vs. connection, etc.)

- Parts of yourself that seemed hidden or suppressed across various situations

What patterns do you see connecting different areas of your life?

Which themes feel most significant or emotionally charged for you?

Step 2: Core Shadow Themes

Based on your pattern identification, write 2-3 sentences that capture your most significant shadow themes. These should be broad enough to encompass multiple life areas but specific enough to feel personally meaningful.

For example:

- "I've learned to hide my natural intensity and emotional depth because I was taught that being 'too much' pushes people away, so I present a controlled, agreeable version of myself while my authentic feelings go underground."

- "I carry deep anxiety about not being good enough, so I overwork and over-give to prove my worth, but this leaves me exhausted and resentful while never actually addressing the underlying insecurity."

What would you say are your 2-3 core shadow themes?

How do these themes create problems or limitations in your life?

What gifts or strengths might be hidden within these shadow patterns?

Step 3: The Shadow Mapping Exercise

Create a visual map of your shadow patterns using whatever format appeals to you—a diagram, mind map, list, or artistic representation. Include:

Center: Your core shadow themes
Branches: How these themes show up in different life areas (work, relationships, family, money, social media)
Connections: Lines or arrows showing how patterns in one area affect others
Hidden Gifts: Positive qualities that might be buried within each shadow pattern
Costs: What these patterns cost you in terms of energy, authenticity, or life satisfaction

What surprises you about seeing your patterns mapped out visually?

Which connections between different life areas feel most significant?

Step 4: The Integration Planning

For each core shadow theme, write about:

- How you want your relationship with this pattern to change

- What it would look like to work with this shadow consciously instead of being controlled by it

- What first steps you could take to begin integrating this aspect of yourself

- What support or resources might help you in this integration process

Which shadow patterns feel most ready for integration work?

What feels most challenging or scary about working with these patterns?

What would be possible in your life if you could work with your shadow consciously?

Reflection Questions

What has been the most surprising discovery from this week's shadow work?

How do your shadow patterns both protect and limit you?

What connections do you see between your current life challenges and your shadow themes?

What would change about your daily experience if you accepted all parts of yourself as valuable?

Understanding Shadow Integration

Integration doesn't mean eliminating your shadow patterns or becoming a completely different person. It means developing a conscious relationship with all aspects of your personality so you can choose how to express them rather than being controlled by unconscious dynamics.

Shadow Acceptance: Recognizing that your shadow patterns developed for good reasons and served important functions, even if they're not serving you optimally now.

Conscious Choice: Being able to choose when and how to express different aspects of your personality based on current circumstances rather than automatic patterns.

Energy Reclamation: Recovering the energy you've been using to suppress or manage shadow aspects and redirecting it toward authentic self-expression.

Wholeness: Operating from your full capacity rather than just the parts of yourself you consider acceptable or safe.

Integration is a gradual process that happens over time through consistent awareness and practice. You don't need to work with all your shadow patterns simultaneously—you can focus on one or two themes while keeping the others in gentle awareness.

Preparing for Deeper Work

This week provided the foundation for the shadow work that continues over the next three weeks. You now have a map of your personal patterns and an understanding of how your shadow operates in daily life. The coming weeks will focus on more specific techniques for working with these patterns consciously.

Some things to remember as you continue:

Progress isn't Linear: You might have days when your shadow patterns feel more prominent or challenging. This doesn't mean you're going backward—it means you're becoming more aware of dynamics that were always there.

Small Changes Matter: Integration happens through small, consistent shifts in awareness and behavior rather than dramatic personality overhauls.

Support is Important: This work can bring up emotions or memories that feel overwhelming. Don't hesitate to reach out to friends, family, or professional support if you need it.

Self-Compassion is Key: Treat yourself with the same kindness you'd show a good friend who was working to understand and improve themselves.

Daily Integration

Today, practice living with awareness of your shadow patterns without trying to fix or change them. When you notice yourself falling into familiar patterns—comparing yourself on social media, overworking to prove your worth, hiding authentic emotions—just acknowledge what's happening without judgment.

This awareness practice is the foundation of all shadow work. Before you can work with patterns consciously, you need to be able to recognize them as they're happening. Today is about strengthening that recognition muscle.

Spend some time with your shadow map, adding to it or modifying it as new insights arise. Consider sharing appropriate parts with trusted friends or family members who might offer supportive perspective on your growth process.

Tomorrow's Preparation

As you enter Week 2, you'll begin looking more specifically at how your shadow patterns formed and how they continue to operate below conscious awareness. Prepare by setting an intention for deeper self-exploration and gathering any additional support resources you might need as the work intensifies.

Having established these coordinates, you're ready to move into more specific excavation work, exploring the historical roots of your patterns and developing practical techniques for working with them in daily life.

Day 8: Climate Anxiety and Future-Fear Shadows

Take a moment to think about the future—not tomorrow or next week, but ten or twenty years from now. What comes up for you? Excitement about possibilities? Anxiety about uncertainty? A feeling of being overwhelmed by forces beyond your control? Whatever arises, notice it without trying to change it right away.

You're probably familiar with that particular knot in your stomach that shows up when you think about climate change, political instability, or economic uncertainty. Maybe you've noticed yourself avoiding news about environmental disasters, or feeling paralyzed when trying to make long-term plans. These reactions aren't character flaws or signs of weakness—they're natural responses to living through a period of unprecedented global uncertainty.

Your generation is the first to grow up knowing that many basic assumptions about the future might not hold true. Previous generations could assume that their children would have similar opportunities, that environmental conditions would remain relatively stable, and that social progress would continue steadily. You don't have those assumptions, and that uncertainty has shaped your psyche in ways that are just beginning to be understood.

Environmental Anxiety and Millennial Development

Climate anxiety isn't just worry about environmental issues—it's a fundamental uncertainty about the future that affects how you approach everything from career decisions to having children. You've watched unprecedented wildfires, floods, and extreme weather events while being told that these are just the beginning of larger changes ahead.

This knowledge arrived during your formative years, when you were developing your basic sense of how the world works and what's possible for your life. Unlike older generations who learned about climate change as adults with already-established worldviews, you integrated this uncertainty into your fundamental assumptions about reality.

The result is that many millennials carry what psychologists call "anticipatory grief"—mourning for losses that haven't happened yet but seem inevitable. You might find yourself grieving for natural places that might disappear, for a stable climate your children might not experience, or for economic opportunities that might not exist in the future.

This grief often operates as a shadow because it's too overwhelming to process consciously. Parts of you that feel hopeless or helpless about the future might get suppressed in order to function in daily life. But these feelings don't disappear—they influence your decisions and energy levels from below conscious awareness.

How Uncertainty Triggers Shadow Responses

Living with chronic uncertainty about the future activates several common shadow patterns that help you cope with feelings of powerlessness:

The Control Shadow: When the big picture feels uncontrollable, you might develop excessive need for control in smaller areas of life. You might become rigid about routines, perfectionist about work projects, or anxious about any deviation from plans.

The Avoidance Shadow: The overwhelm of global challenges can lead to avoiding news, environmental topics, or long-term planning altogether. You might find yourself unable to think about the future without anxiety, so you focus exclusively on immediate concerns.

The Despair Shadow: Parts of you that feel hopeless about the future might go underground, showing up as chronic low-level depression, difficulty getting excited about goals, or a sense that nothing you do matters anyway.

The Hypervigilance Shadow: Constant awareness of potential disasters can create chronic stress responses, where you're always scanning for threats and unable to fully relax even during safe, pleasant experiences.

One person described their climate anxiety shadow: "I realized I'd stopped making long-term plans because the future felt too uncertain. I wasn't saving for retirement, wasn't thinking about having kids, wasn't even booking vacations more than a few months in advance. I told myself I was being realistic, but I was actually letting fear make all my decisions."

The Millennial Future-Fear Phenomenon

Beyond environmental concerns, your generation faces several types of future uncertainty that previous generations didn't experience at the same scale:

Economic Instability: You've witnessed multiple economic disruptions, seen traditional career paths become unreliable, and watched housing costs outpace income growth. The economic security that previous generations took for granted feels uncertain for many millennials.

Technological Disruption: The pace of technological change means that the skills and industries that are valuable today might be obsolete in a decade. This creates anxiety about career planning and professional identity.

Social Fragmentation: Political polarization, social media echo chambers, and declining trust in institutions create uncertainty about social stability and shared values.

Global Interconnectedness: You're more aware than previous generations of global challenges, conflicts, and disasters because of constant media coverage and social media. This creates a sense of responsibility for problems that feel too large for individual action.

These uncertainties interact to create what researchers call "future shock"—a psychological state where the rate of change exceeds your ability to adapt emotionally. Parts of your personality that need predictability and security might go into hiding when the external world feels too chaotic to provide either.

Exercise: Future Fear Exploration

This exercise helps you identify specific ways that uncertainty about the future affects your current choices and emotional well-being.

Step 1: The Future Scenario Assessment

Write about your honest feelings when you imagine different future scenarios. For each area, include both your hopes and your fears:

- Environmental conditions 10-20 years from now

- Economic opportunities for your generation

- Social and political stability in your lifetime

- Your personal financial security and retirement prospects

- The world you might leave for future children

Which scenarios generate the most anxiety or hopelessness for you?

How do these feelings affect your current life decisions?

Step 2: The Avoidance Pattern Recognition

Think about ways you might be avoiding engagement with future-focused topics or decisions. Consider:

- News topics or conversations you consistently avoid

- Long-term planning tasks you keep putting off

- Financial or career decisions you're postponing

- Conversations about having children or major life commitments

- Activities or purchases you avoid because "what's the point?"

What patterns do you notice in what you avoid thinking about?

How might these avoidance patterns be protecting you from overwhelming feelings?

Step 3: The Control Compensation Analysis

Identify areas where you might be over-controlling as a way to manage feelings of powerlessness about larger issues:

- Daily routines that feel rigid or compulsive

- Work or personal projects where you demand perfection

- Relationships where you need excessive reassurance or predictability

- Lifestyle choices focused primarily on risk minimization

How might these control patterns be connected to anxiety about uncontrollable future events?

What would happen if you loosened some of this control without addressing the underlying anxiety?

Step 4: The Hope and Agency Inventory

Write about areas where you still feel hopeful and empowered about the future:

- Issues where you believe individual action can make a difference

- Aspects of your personal future that excite or motivate you

- Examples of positive change you've witnessed or contributed to

- Skills, relationships, or resources you have that feel valuable regardless of future uncertainty

What supports your sense of hope and personal agency?

How might you strengthen these resources?

Reflection Questions

How has awareness of global challenges affected your approach to personal goal-setting?

What would you pursue if you knew the future would be stable and positive?

How do you balance staying informed about important issues with protecting your mental health?

What gives you a sense of meaning and purpose despite uncertainty about the future?

Building Resilience Practices

Working with future-fear shadows doesn't mean becoming naive about global challenges or forcing yourself to feel optimistic about difficult realities. It means developing the emotional resilience to engage with uncertainty without being paralyzed by it.

Present-Moment Anchoring: When anxiety about the future becomes overwhelming, practice returning attention to current experiences. What do you actually know about today? What's working in your life right now? What can you appreciate in this moment?

Sphere of Influence Focus: Distinguish between issues you can influence and those you can't. Put most of your emotional energy into areas where your actions can make a difference, while staying informed about larger issues without trying to solve them personally.

Community Connection: Find ways to connect with others who share your concerns and values. Isolation increases anxiety about the future, while community provides both emotional support and practical collaboration opportunities.

Meaningful Action: Identify specific actions you can take that align with your values and contribute to positive change, even if the impact feels small. Action often reduces anxiety better than planning or worrying.

Flexible Planning: Develop planning approaches that account for uncertainty rather than assuming predictability. This might mean having multiple backup plans, focusing on adaptable skills, or setting shorter-term goals that can be adjusted as conditions change.

Working with Climate Grief

If you're experiencing grief about environmental loss or climate change, that grief deserves recognition and processing rather than suppression. Climate grief is a rational response to real losses and threats, not a psychological problem to eliminate.

Acknowledge the Reality: It's appropriate to feel sad about environmental destruction, species loss, and climate impacts. These feelings show that you care about something valuable.

Share the Burden: This grief is too large for any individual to carry alone. Find others who understand these concerns and can provide emotional support.

Channel into Action: Grief often contains energy that can be directed toward meaningful action. Consider what climate-related activities align with your skills and interests.

Practice Acceptance: You can care deeply about environmental issues while accepting that you can't single-handedly solve climate change. Your role is to contribute what you can, not to carry responsibility for global outcomes.

Daily Integration

Today, practice noticing when future anxiety influences your current decisions or emotional state. When you find yourself avoiding news, procrastinating on long-term planning, or feeling overwhelmed by global issues, get curious about what specific fears or feelings are being triggered.

Also experiment with balancing awareness and action. Choose one small, concrete action you can take today that aligns with your values regarding future challenges. This might be a financial decision, an environmental choice, a community connection, or a self-care practice that builds resilience.

Remember that feeling anxious about legitimate threats isn't pathological—it's intelligent. The goal isn't to eliminate anxiety about the future, but to work with it skillfully so it informs your choices without paralyzing you.

Tomorrow's Preparation

Pay attention today to interactions where you feel pressure to meet others' needs or expectations at the expense of your own preferences. Notice how you respond when people seem disappointed in you or when you have the opportunity to help someone. These observations will help us explore people-pleasing patterns tomorrow.

This groundwork opens several pathways to explore how you've learned to manage relationships by managing others' emotions, another common shadow pattern that developed as a protective strategy during uncertain times.

Day 9: The People-Pleasing Millennial Epidemic

Daily Check-In

Before interacting with anyone today, take a moment to check in with your own needs, preferences, and energy levels. What do you actually want from your day? What would feel genuinely caring toward yourself? Now notice what happens when you imagine prioritizing these authentic desires over other people's expectations or needs.

You've probably found yourself agreeing to plans you don't actually want, staying late at work to help colleagues when you're exhausted, or crafting text messages to avoid any possibility of disappointing someone. Maybe you've noticed that you know more about your friends' problems than they know about yours, or that you feel guilty whenever you're not being helpful to somebody.

These patterns aren't necessarily problems, but they become shadows when they're automatic rather than conscious choices. Many millennials developed particularly strong people-pleasing patterns because you came of age during a time when social approval felt both more important and more fragile than it had for previous generations.

The Self-Esteem Generation and Its Consequences

Your generation was raised during the height of the self-esteem movement, when parents, teachers, and other adults worked hard to make children feel valued and special. This well-intentioned approach created some unexpected psychological dynamics that continue to influence millennial behavior in adulthood.

Growing up with constant positive reinforcement, many millennials learned to equate their worth with others' approval. You received praise not just for achievements but for being good, helpful, and considerate. This created a psychological dependency on external validation that can make authentic self-advocacy feel dangerous or selfish.

Additionally, you were often protected from experiences of disappointment, conflict, or failure that help children develop emotional resilience. While this protection was loving, it sometimes left millennials without skills for handling disapproval or interpersonal tension. People-pleasing becomes a way to avoid triggering these uncomfortable feelings in yourself or others.

One person realized this connection: "I got so much praise growing up for being mature, helpful, and easy-going that I thought those were my best qualities. But I realized I never learned how to handle conflict or disappointment. Even as an adult, if someone seems upset with me, I panic and immediately try to fix it, even when their feelings aren't actually my responsibility."

Millennial People-Pleasing Patterns

People-pleasing shows up differently for millennials than it did for previous generations because you developed these patterns in unique social and economic conditions:

Digital People-Pleasing: Social media created new ways to seek approval and avoid disapproval. You might carefully craft posts to generate positive responses, avoid sharing opinions that might be controversial, or feel anxious when your content doesn't receive expected engagement.

Economic People-Pleasing: Job insecurity and competitive work environments can intensify people-pleasing at work. You might take on excessive responsibilities, avoid advocating for yourself, or prioritize being liked over being respected.

Relationship People-Pleasing: Dating apps and changing social norms create pressure to be the ideal partner while hiding authentic needs. You might suppress preferences about pace, commitment, or boundaries to avoid seeming demanding or high-maintenance.

Family People-Pleasing: Economic pressures might keep you dependent on family support longer than previous generations, making it feel unsafe to disappoint parents or assert independence around lifestyle choices.

The Shadow Side of Being "Nice"

People-pleasing patterns often develop from genuine kindness and consideration for others, but they become shadows when they require suppressing authentic parts of yourself. The "nice" persona that many millennials developed can hide:

Natural Assertiveness: Your ability to advocate for yourself, set boundaries, and express disagreement might go underground if it conflicts with being agreeable and helpful.

Genuine Preferences: Your actual likes, dislikes, opinions, and desires might become unclear to you if you've spent years prioritizing others' preferences over your own.

Healthy Selfishness: Your legitimate needs for rest, recognition, personal time, and reciprocal relationships might feel selfish if you've learned that caring for yourself is less important than caring for others.

Authentic Emotions: Feelings like anger, disappointment, jealousy, or frustration might get suppressed if they conflict with maintaining a positive, supportive persona.

The irony is that people-pleasing often creates the rejection it's trying to avoid. When you consistently hide your authentic personality, people respond to a performance rather than the real you. This can lead to relationships that feel hollow or one-sided, reinforcing the belief that you need to earn love through helpful behavior.

Excrcise: People-Pleasing Pattern Recognition

This exercise helps you identify specific ways that people-pleasing patterns operate in your life and what authentic needs or desires they might be covering.

Step 1: The People-Pleasing Audit

Think about your interactions over the past week and identify times when you prioritized others' comfort over your own authentic preferences. Consider:

- Conversations where you agreed with opinions you don't actually share

- Social invitations you accepted despite not wanting to go

- Work tasks you took on when you were already overwhelmed

- Times you avoided expressing disappointment, frustration, or disagreement

- Situations where you gave advice or help when you needed support yourself

What patterns do you notice in when and with whom you people-please most?

How did you feel in your body during these interactions?

Step 2: The Authentic Desire Inventory

For each people-pleasing situation you identified, write about what you would have preferred to do or say if you weren't concerned about others' reactions:

- What was your honest opinion in those conversations?

- How would you have preferred to spend your time instead of those social obligations?

- What work boundaries would you have set if you weren't worried about seeming unhelpful?

- What emotions would you have expressed if you felt safe to be authentic?

- What support would you have asked for instead of always providing it?

What themes emerge in your authentic desires?

How much energy do you spend managing others' emotions versus attending to your own?

Step 3: The Approval Anxiety Assessment

Write about what you imagine would happen if you stopped people-pleasing in specific relationships or situations:

- How do you think people would respond if you expressed disagreement more often?

- What fears come up when you imagine setting firmer boundaries?

- How might your relationships change if you were more honest about your needs?

- What stories do you tell yourself about what makes you loveable or valuable to others?

Which fears about authenticity feel realistic versus which feel like inherited programming?

How might some of your people-pleasing actually prevent deeper connection?

Step 4: The Cost-Benefit Analysis

For your main people-pleasing patterns, honestly assess both the benefits and costs:

Benefits might include:

- Avoiding conflict or disappointment

- Feeling needed and valued

- Maintaining harmony in relationships

- Getting approval and positive feedback

Costs might include:

- Exhaustion from constantly managing others' emotions
- Resentment about one-sided relationships
- Confusion about your own preferences and needs
- Anxiety about authenticity and potential rejection

How do the costs and benefits balance out for you?

Which people-pleasing patterns feel worth keeping versus which feel ready to change?

Reflection Questions

How has your definition of being a "good person" influenced your relationship patterns?

What would change about your relationships if you believed people could love you while occasionally being disappointed by your choices?

How do you distinguish between genuine generosity and compulsive people-pleasing?

What would it mean to be equally committed to your own well-being as you are to others'?

Authentic Relationship Building

Moving beyond automatic people-pleasing doesn't mean becoming selfish or inconsiderate. It means developing relationships based on mutual authenticity rather than one-sided caretaking. Authentic relationships can handle disappointment, disagreement, and individual differences because they're built on genuine connection rather than performance.

Gradual Authenticity: Start expressing your authentic preferences in low-stakes situations. Notice that most people can handle your honest opinions without rejecting you entirely.

Reciprocity Assessment: Pay attention to which relationships involve mutual care and support versus which ones drain your energy without providing emotional reciprocity.

Boundary Practice: Set small boundaries around your time, energy, and emotional availability. Notice that healthy people respect boundaries rather than punishing you for having them.

Direct Communication: Practice expressing needs, preferences, and feelings directly rather than hoping others will guess or anticipate them. Many people appreciate clarity over having to interpret subtle cues.

Conflict Tolerance: Develop comfort with disappointing people occasionally. Most relationships can survive disagreement and disappointment if the underlying connection is genuine.

Kindness and People-Pleasing

Real kindness comes from choosing to care for others from a place of personal fullness rather than empty obligation. People-pleasing often creates resentment because it requires self-abandonment. Learning the difference helps you maintain your natural generosity while protecting your authentic self.

Genuine Kindness feels energizing, comes from free choice, includes appropriate boundaries, and allows for reciprocity. You can be kind while occasionally disappointing people.

Compulsive People-Pleasing feels draining, comes from obligation or fear, involves sacrifice of authentic needs, and often creates one-sided relationships. You avoid disappointing others at the cost of disappointing yourself.

Healthy Selfishness means taking care of your legitimate needs so you can show up authentically in relationships. This actually makes you more available for genuine connection because you're not constantly managing resentment or depletion.

Daily Integration

Today, practice making small choices based on your authentic preferences rather than anticipated reactions from others. This might mean expressing a genuine opinion in conversation, declining a social obligation you don't want, or asking for support instead of always providing it.

Pay attention to the difference between how you feel when you're being authentic versus when you're managing others' emotions. Notice that many people appreciate honesty and directness more than constant agreeability.

Also practice tolerating other people's disappointment when it arises. Most disappointment passes quickly when it's not fed by excessive accommodation or apologizing.

Tomorrow's Preparation

As you go through your day, notice moments when you feel pressure to be perfect, productive, or impressive. Pay attention to internal criticism when you make mistakes or when your performance doesn't meet your own standards. These observations will help us explore perfectionism and achievement shadows tomorrow.

From this vantage point, you can begin to see how people-pleasing connects to other shadow patterns, particularly the perfectionist tendencies that often drive both the need for approval and the fear of making mistakes.

Day 10: Instagram Perfectionism and Achievement Addiction

Daily Check-In

Before looking at your phone or checking any social media today, pause and notice your internal state. How do you feel about yourself right now, before comparing your life to anyone else's curated highlights? What's your honest assessment of your current achievements, productivity, and overall life progress?

You probably know the feeling of spending twenty minutes crafting the perfect caption for a photo that took thirty seconds to experience. Or maybe you've caught yourself researching the "optimal posting time" for maximum engagement, or feeling genuinely disappointed when a post you worked on doesn't get the response you expected. These behaviors aren't vanity—they're symptoms of a deeper psychological pattern where your worth feels tied to external validation and perfect performance.

Your generation grew up during the intersection of the achievement culture and social media emergence, creating a perfect storm for perfectionist shadows. You learned to optimize not just your actual accomplishments but your presentation of those accomplishments, often spending more energy managing your image than enjoying your experiences.

Social Media Perfectionism Culture

Instagram, Facebook, and other platforms created a new type of social pressure that no previous generation experienced. Every experience became a potential performance, every moment a possible content opportunity. You learned to see your life through the lens of how it might appear to others, developing an internal social media manager who constantly evaluates experiences for their shareability.

This created several psychological dynamics that previous generations didn't have to navigate:

The Curation Pressure: Every aspect of life becomes subject to editing and optimization. You might choose restaurants based on their photo potential, plan outfits considering how they'll look in pictures, or avoid sharing experiences that don't fit your personal brand.

The Metrics Anxiety: Likes, comments, shares, and followers become quantified measures of social approval. You might check these metrics compulsively, feel deflated when posts underperform, or avoid posting when you're not confident about potential engagement.

The Comparison Trap: You're exposed to thousands of people's highlight reels daily, creating constant opportunities for unfavorable comparison. Someone is always having more fun, looking more attractive, achieving more success, or living more adventurously than you appear to be.

The Authenticity Paradox: Pressure to be "authentic" online creates performance of authenticity, where even vulnerability becomes calculated for optimal response. You might share struggles in ways designed to generate support rather than genuine expression of experience.

One person described their social media perfectionism: "I realized I was living my life twice—once while I was having the experience, and again when I was figuring out how to present it online. I spent vacation dinners thinking about captions instead of enjoying conversations. I was optimizing my life for strangers on the internet instead of actually living it."

The Achievement Shadow in Competitive Times

Beyond social media perfectionism, many millennials developed achievement addiction as a response to economic uncertainty and competitive educational environments. When traditional paths to success became less reliable, achievement itself became a way to manage anxiety about the future.

The Productivity Obsession: You might feel guilty during downtime, judge your days by how much you accomplished, or treat rest as something that must be earned through sufficient productivity. Your worth feels tied to output rather than inherent value.

The Optimization Compulsion: Every area of life becomes a project to improve. You might track sleep, optimize nutrition, hack your productivity, and treat self-care as another item on your achievement list rather than genuine nurturing.

The Milestone Anxiety: Traditional life milestones become sources of stress rather than celebration. You might feel behind if you're not meeting social expectations about career progress, relationship status, or lifestyle achievements by certain ages.

The Impostor Syndrome Cycle: High achievement standards combined with social media comparison create chronic feelings of inadequacy. No matter what you accomplish, it never feels like enough because you're always aware of others who appear to be doing more or better.

Exercise: Perfectionist Shadow Dialogue

This exercise helps you identify your specific perfectionist patterns and have a conversation with the parts of yourself that drive these behaviors.

Step 1: The Perfectionism Assessment

Write about areas of your life where you notice perfectionist tendencies. Consider:

- Social media posting and image curation

- Work projects and professional presentation

- Physical appearance and health habits

- Home organization and lifestyle presentation

- Learning new skills or hobbies

- Relationship dynamics and communication

In which areas do you spend excessive time trying to get things "just right"?

Where do you avoid starting things because you're worried about imperfect outcomes?

Step 2: The Achievement Motivation Analysis

For your main perfectionist patterns, explore what you're hoping to achieve or avoid:

- What are you hoping other people will think about you?

- What feelings are you trying to avoid (rejection, criticism, failure, insignificance)?

- What do you believe perfect performance will get you?

- What do you fear will happen if you're imperfect or mediocre?

Which motivations feel authentic to your values versus driven by anxiety or insecurity?

How much energy do you spend trying to control others' perceptions of you?

Step 3: The Perfectionist Dialogue

Write a conversation between two parts of yourself: the perfectionist part and the part that wants to relax standards. Let each part explain its perspective without judgment.

Perfectionist part: "We need to maintain high standards because..."

Relaxed part: "But that's exhausting and it prevents us from..."

Continue this dialogue, letting each part respond authentically to the other's concerns.

What does the perfectionist part want that's actually legitimate?

What is the relaxed part trying to protect or provide?

How might both parts' needs be honored without the compulsive quality?

Step 4: The "Good Enough" Experiment Planning

Choose one area where you could experiment with "good enough" standards instead of perfection. Consider:

- Social media posts you could share without extensive editing

- Work projects you could complete efficiently rather than perfectly

- Social interactions where you could be more authentic and less polished

- Creative activities you could do for enjoyment rather than achievement

What would it look like to do this activity with 80% effort instead of 100%?

What are you afraid would happen if you lowered your standards in this area?

How might "good enough" actually serve you better than perfection in this situation?

Reflection Questions

How has social media changed your relationship with your own experiences and achievements?

What would you pursue if you knew no one would see or judge the results?

How do you distinguish between healthy high standards and compulsive perfectionism?

What would change about your daily experience if you believed you were already enough as you are?

Embracing "Good Enough" Mentality

Moving beyond perfectionism doesn't mean lowering all standards or becoming careless about quality. It means choosing consciously where to invest perfectionist energy and where to accept good enough, based on what actually matters to you rather than anxiety about others' judgments.

Strategic Perfectionism: Reserve perfectionist effort for areas that genuinely matter to your values and goals. Maybe you care deeply about your work quality but not about having a perfectly organized home, or vice versa.

Process Over Product: Focus on enjoying activities rather than optimizing outcomes. The value of experiences isn't just in how they turn out but in what you learn and how they make you feel during the process.

Experimentation Over Perfection: Give yourself permission to try things badly. Most skills require practice and mistakes before they become satisfying. Perfectionism often prevents starting rather than ensuring good results.

Authenticity Over Image: Let your actual personality show rather than presenting a curated version of yourself. Most people prefer authentic connection over impressive performance.

Progress Over Perfection: Celebrate incremental improvement rather than demanding immediate mastery. Small, consistent efforts often create better results than sporadic perfect attempts.

Working with Achievement Addiction

If you recognize achievement addiction patterns, the goal isn't to stop achieving but to change your relationship with achievement. Healthy achievement feels energizing and aligns with your values. Compulsive achievement feels driven by anxiety and creates more pressure than satisfaction.

Internal Validation: Practice appreciating your efforts and progress rather than only celebrating external recognition. Can you feel good about your work even when others don't notice it?

Intrinsic Motivation: Reconnect with activities you enjoy for their own sake rather than what they might get you. What do you like to do when no one is watching or measuring?

Rest as Resistance: Practice doing nothing productive sometimes, just because you're a human being who deserves rest regardless of what you've accomplished.

Failure as Information: Treat mistakes and failures as data about what doesn't work rather than evidence of personal inadequacy. What can you learn from imperfect outcomes?

Daily Integration

Today, practice choosing "good enough" in at least one situation where you would normally aim for perfection. Notice what happens when you post a photo without excessive filtering, send an email without rewriting it multiple times, or complete a task efficiently rather than perfectly.

Pay attention to the difference between intrinsic satisfaction and external validation. When do you feel genuinely pleased with your efforts versus when do you feel dependent on others' responses?

Also notice your internal dialogue about productivity and achievement. Are you encouraging yourself the way you'd encourage a good friend, or are you more critical and demanding?

Tomorrow's Preparation

As you interact with others today, pay attention to moments when you feel annoyed, frustrated, or angry but don't express these feelings directly. Notice what happens to that energy—does it get suppressed, redirected, or expressed indirectly? These observations will help us explore anger and conflict avoidance patterns tomorrow.

With these pieces in place, you're ready to examine one of the most commonly suppressed emotions in millennial culture: anger, and how learning to avoid conflict can create shadow patterns that undermine authentic relationships.

Day 11: Suppressed Anger in Conflict-Averse Culture

Daily Check-In

Before reading any further, take a moment to notice how you feel when you imagine someone being genuinely angry with you—not just disappointed or annoyed, but actually mad. What happens in your body? Do you feel anxious, defensive, or eager to fix the situation immediately? Now imagine expressing real anger toward someone else. Does that feel natural and acceptable, or scary and uncomfortable?

You've probably been praised your whole life for being easy-going, understanding, and mature. Maybe you pride yourself on being someone who "doesn't do drama" or who can stay calm in difficult situations. These are valuable qualities, but they can become shadows when they require you to suppress legitimate anger or avoid necessary conflicts.

Many millennials learned to be conflict-averse during childhood, often because your families were dealing with economic stress, divorce, or other challenges that made additional tension feel dangerous. You might have learned that expressing anger caused problems rather than solved them, so parts of your natural assertiveness went underground.

Millennial Conflict Avoidance Patterns

Your generation grew up during a cultural shift toward valuing emotional intelligence, communication skills, and collaborative problem-solving. These developments created healthier ways to handle disagreement, but they also sometimes led to viewing any form of direct confrontation as problematic or immature.

Additionally, social media culture emphasizes positivity and agreeableness. Expressing anger online often leads to backlash or public shaming, so you learned early that controversial or aggressive emotions should be kept private. This reinforced patterns of suppressing anger rather than learning to express it constructively.

Economic uncertainty also contributed to conflict avoidance patterns. When job security feels fragile and family support might be necessary longer than expected, expressing anger toward authority figures or family members can feel risky. You might have learned to prioritize keeping peace over advocating for yourself.

The result is that many millennials developed what psychologists call "anger phobia"—not just discomfort with others' anger, but anxiety about their own anger and confusion about when and how to express it appropriately.

The Shadow Side of Being "Chill"

The "chill" persona that many millennials cultivated often masks significant emotional intensity that had to go underground. When you consistently present yourself as laid-back and drama-free, several authentic aspects of your personality might become shadows:

Natural Assertiveness: Your ability to advocate for yourself, express disagreement, and stand firm on important issues might be suppressed if it conflicts with being agreeable and low-maintenance.

Protective Instincts: Your capacity to defend yourself and others when boundaries are violated might go underground if it's seen as creating unnecessary conflict or being too aggressive.

Passionate Intensity: Your strong feelings about injustice, values, or important issues might be toned down if expressing them feels like being "too much" or causing drama.

Competitive Drive: Your natural competitiveness and desire to win might be hidden if it doesn't match cultural expectations about collaboration and emotional intelligence.

91

One person recognized their anger shadow: "I always thought I was just naturally calm and rational, but I realized I was actually terrified of conflict. I would agree to things that bothered me, let people treat me poorly, and then feel resentful but confused about why. I had suppressed my anger so completely that I didn't even know when I was upset until it built up into anxiety or depression."

Passive-Aggression as Shadow Expression

When anger can't be expressed directly, it often emerges indirectly through passive-aggressive behaviors. Passive-aggression allows you to express frustration while maintaining plausible deniability about being angry. Common forms include:

The Silent Treatment: Withdrawing emotionally or physically when upset instead of addressing the issue directly.

Sarcasm and Subtle Digs: Making comments that express irritation through humor or indirect criticism.

Procrastination and "Forgetting": Avoiding tasks or commitments as a way to express resistance without direct confrontation.

Chronic Lateness: Being consistently late to commitments with people you're angry with while being punctual with others.

Social Media Subposting: Making vague posts about being frustrated without identifying the source of your anger.

Excessive Agreeability: Saying yes to requests while internal resentment builds, then eventually exploding or withdrawing completely.

Passive-aggression often feels like the only safe way to express anger, but it usually creates more relationship problems than direct communication would. People can sense indirect hostility even when they can't identify it explicitly, leading to confusion and escalated tension.

Exercise: Anger Archaeology

This exercise helps you identify where your natural anger and assertiveness have been suppressed and how those emotions might be expressing themselves indirectly.

Step 1: The Anger History Assessment

Think about your relationship with anger throughout your life. Write about:

- How anger was handled in your family growing up
- Messages you received about expressing disagreement or frustration
- Times when expressing anger led to negative consequences
- People in your life who you learned not to be angry with
- Situations where you learned that being upset caused more problems

What did you learn about when and how it's acceptable to be angry?

How did these early experiences shape your current relationship with anger?

Step 2: The Suppressed Anger Inventory

Think about current situations that frustrate or upset you but that you haven't addressed directly. Consider:

- Work situations where you feel unappreciated or treated unfairly
- Relationships where you give more than you receive
- Family dynamics that drain your energy or violate your boundaries
- Social situations where you feel disrespected or dismissed

- Global issues that make you feel angry but powerless

Which situations generate the most unexpressed anger for you?

How do you typically handle these feelings when they come up?

Step 3: The Passive-Aggressive Pattern Recognition

Honestly assess ways you might express anger indirectly. Consider:

- Times when you've withdrawn from people instead of addressing conflicts
- Situations where you've used sarcasm or subtle criticism
- Instances of procrastination or "forgetting" when upset with someone
- Social media posts that expressed frustration without naming the source
- Ways you might withhold cooperation or enthusiasm when feeling unappreciated

What patterns do you notice in how you express anger indirectly?

How might these indirect expressions create confusion or escalated conflict?

Step 4: The Direct Anger Experiment Planning

Choose one situation where you could experiment with expressing anger more directly and constructively. Consider:

- A boundary that needs to be set with someone in your life
- A workplace issue that affects your well-being or effectiveness
- A recurring relationship dynamic that frustrates you
- A family situation where you consistently compromise your needs

What would it look like to address this situation with direct, honest communication?

What are you afraid might happen if you express anger about this issue?

How might the relationship or situation improve if you addressed it directly?

Reflection Questions

How do you distinguish between healthy conflict avoidance and problematic anger suppression?

What would change about your relationships if you believed anger could be expressed constructively?

How might your natural assertiveness be a strength rather than something to manage or hide?

What would it mean to be as committed to your own needs as you are to maintaining peace?

Healthy Anger Expression Techniques

Learning to work with anger constructively doesn't mean becoming aggressive or creating unnecessary drama. It means developing skills for expressing frustration and setting boundaries in ways that strengthen rather than damage relationships.

Anger as Information: Anger often signals that a boundary has been crossed, a need isn't being met, or a value is being violated. Instead of suppressing the emotion, get curious about what it's telling you about the situation.

Direct Communication: Practice expressing anger through "I" statements that describe your experience rather than accusations about others' behavior. "I feel frustrated when..." rather than "You always..."

Boundary Setting: Use anger energy to establish and maintain healthy boundaries rather than accommodating behavior that violates your limits. Anger can fuel necessary self-protection.

Timing and Setting: Choose appropriate times and places for difficult conversations. Anger doesn't always need to be expressed immediately, but it shouldn't be suppressed indefinitely.

Physical Release: Find healthy ways to discharge anger energy through exercise, creative expression, or physical activities before having important conversations.

Conflict as Connection: Reframe conflict as an opportunity to understand each other better and strengthen relationships rather than something to avoid at all costs.

Working with Anger Anxiety

If expressing anger feels scary or dangerous, start small and build confidence gradually. Most people can handle direct communication about problems better than the confusion created by indirect expression.

Practice with Low Stakes: Begin expressing minor frustrations in relationships that feel safe before addressing major issues or dealing with intimidating people.

Prepare for Reactions: People might be surprised if you start expressing anger after years of being accommodating. Give them time to adjust to your more authentic communication style.

Expect Initial Discomfort: Expressing anger directly might feel awkward or intense at first. This is normal when you're developing new emotional skills.

Set Realistic Expectations: Not every expression of anger will lead to resolution or change. Sometimes the value is in honoring your own experience rather than controlling outcomes.

Daily Integration

Today, practice noticing when you feel annoyed, frustrated, or angry without immediately trying to suppress or redirect those feelings. Get curious about what your anger might be telling you about the situation and whether any action might be appropriate.

Also pay attention to passive-aggressive impulses when they arise. Before withdrawing, being sarcastic, or "forgetting" commitments, consider whether there's a more direct way to address whatever is bothering you.

Remember that learning to work with anger is a skill that develops over time. You don't need to become confrontational overnight, but you can start honoring your authentic emotional responses rather than automatically suppressing them.

Tomorrow's Preparation

As you go through your day, notice moments when you think about creative activities, artistic expression, or projects you used to enjoy. Pay attention to how you feel when you consider pursuing creative interests—excitement, guilt, impracticality? These observations will help us explore the creative shadows that often develop when artistic pursuits conflict with economic survival needs.

These building blocks enable us to explore another crucial area where authentic self-expression often gets suppressed: creativity, and how economic pressures can create internal conflicts about pursuing artistic interests and creative fulfillment.

Day 12: Creative Dreams vs. Economic Survival Reality

Daily Check-In

Take a moment to think about something you used to create for pure enjoyment—drawing, writing, music, crafts, cooking, or any form of artistic expression. When was the last time you engaged with that activity? When you consider making time for creative projects now, what thoughts or feelings come up? Notice whether excitement, guilt, practicality concerns, or something else dominates your response.

You probably used to have creative hobbies that brought you joy without needing to justify their existence. Maybe you wrote stories, played music, made art, or built things just because you enjoyed the process. Then somewhere along the way, these activities started feeling impractical, self-indulgent, or like luxuries you couldn't afford given your adult responsibilities.

Many millennials have creative shadows—artistic interests and expressive impulses that went underground when economic survival became the primary focus. This creates internal conflict between the parts of you that need creative fulfillment and the parts that prioritize financial security and practical achievement.

The Gig Economy and Creative Sacrifice

Your generation entered adulthood during a time when creative industries became increasingly competitive and financially unstable. The advice to "follow your passion" collided with economic realities where artistic careers often require family financial support, unpaid internships, or years of uncertainty that many millennials couldn't afford.

At the same time, the gig economy emerged, promising creative freedom and entrepreneurial opportunities. But many creative professionals discovered that turning art into business often diminished the joy and authenticity that made creativity fulfilling in the first place.

This created what psychologists call "creative dissonance"—internal conflict between your artistic nature and economic pressures. You might have learned to see creativity as impractical, self-indulgent, or something to pursue only after achieving financial stability. But suppressing creative impulses often leads to depression, restlessness, and a sense that something essential is missing from life.

The cultural message became: "Creative pursuits are wonderful, but you need to be practical first." This implied that creativity and financial responsibility were mutually exclusive rather than potentially complementary aspects of a fulfilling life.

The Artist vs. Practical Adult Split

Many millennials developed an internal split between their "artistic self" and their "practical adult self," as if these were incompatible identities rather than different aspects of the same person. This creates several shadow patterns:

The Starving Artist Myth: You might believe that pursuing creativity means accepting poverty or instability, so you avoid artistic activities entirely rather than finding sustainable ways to integrate them into your life.

The Sellout Fear: Conversely, you might believe that making money from creative work corrupts artistic integrity, so you keep creativity completely separate from practical considerations.

The All-or-Nothing Trap: You might think you need to be a professional artist or not create at all, dismissing the value of creative activities that don't generate income or recognition.

The Talent Excuse: You might convince yourself you're "not creative" or lack artistic talent as a way to avoid the discomfort of wanting something that feels impractical or risky.

One person described their creative shadow: "I used to write constantly in college—poetry, short stories, even started a novel. But after graduation, I felt like I needed to focus on my career and adult responsibilities. I told myself I'd get back to writing once I was financially stable, but years passed and I never did. I realized I was treating creativity like a luxury instead of recognizing it as part of what makes me feel alive."

Exercise: Creative Shadow Liberation

This exercise helps you identify how your relationship with creativity has changed over time and explore ways to reintegrate artistic expression into your current life.

Step 1: The Creative History Assessment

Write about your relationship with creativity throughout different life stages:

- What creative activities did you enjoy as a child?

- How did your artistic interests evolve during adolescence and young adulthood?

- When did you start feeling pressure to be more "practical" about career choices?

- What messages did you receive about the viability of creative careers?

- How has your creative expression changed since entering the workforce?

What patterns do you notice in when and why your creative interests became less prominent?

Which creative activities used to bring you the most joy and fulfillment?

Step 2: The Practical vs. Creative Conflict Analysis

Explore the internal conflicts between your creative interests and practical concerns:

- What fears come up when you consider pursuing creative projects?

- How do you rationalize not having time or energy for artistic activities?

- What do you believe about the relationship between creativity and financial responsibility?

- How much of your creative avoidance is based on real constraints versus inherited beliefs?

Which practical concerns about creativity feel legitimate versus which feel like excuses?

How might your creative interests actually complement rather than compete with your practical goals?

Step 3: The Creative Identity Exploration

Write about who you might be if creative expression was a regular part of your life:

- What would you create if time and money weren't factors?

- How might you feel different if you honored your artistic impulses?

- What would your daily or weekly routine include if creativity was a priority?

- How might creative fulfillment affect other areas of your life?

What aspects of yourself feel unexpressed when creativity is absent from your life?

How might your creative interests connect to your values and sense of purpose?

Step 4: The Integration Experiment Planning

Choose one small way you could begin reintegrating creativity into your current life:

- A creative activity you could do for 15-30 minutes weekly

- A artistic project that aligns with your current schedule and resources

- A way to bring more creative expression into your existing work or responsibilities

- A creative community or class you could join for social support and accountability

What would it look like to pursue this creative activity without needing to justify its practicality?

How might you protect this creative time from the pressure to be productive or profitable?

Reflection Questions

How has your definition of "practical" changed since you were younger, and how has this affected your relationship with creativity?

What would it mean to treat creative expression as essential to your well-being rather than optional?

How might engaging with creativity actually support your practical goals rather than competing with them?

What would you create if you knew no one would judge it and you didn't need to make money from it?

Balancing Creativity with Financial Needs

Integrating creativity into your life doesn't require choosing between artistic fulfillment and financial security. Many millennials have found sustainable ways to honor both their creative nature and their practical needs:

Creative Hobbies: Pursue artistic activities for personal enjoyment without pressure to monetize them. Sometimes the value of creativity is the process itself rather than any external outcome.

Creative Problem-Solving: Find ways to bring creative thinking into your existing work or responsibilities. Most jobs benefit from innovative approaches and artistic sensibilities.

Side Projects: Develop creative projects alongside your primary income source, allowing artistic interests to grow gradually without financial pressure.

Creative Community: Connect with others who share your artistic interests, providing mutual support and inspiration for maintaining creative practices.

Hybrid Careers: Look for work that combines practical skills with creative elements, or that provides enough flexibility and income to support artistic pursuits.

Seasonal Creativity: Recognize that creative focus might ebb and flow with other life demands. This doesn't mean abandoning creativity, just accepting natural cycles.

Working with Creative Guilt

Many millennials feel guilty about spending time or money on creative activities, seeing them as self-indulgent when practical concerns demand attention. But creativity often provides psychological benefits that actually support your ability to handle practical responsibilities:

Stress Relief: Creative activities can provide healthy stress release and emotional regulation, improving your capacity for work and relationships.

Problem-Solving Skills: Artistic thinking develops cognitive flexibility and innovative approaches that benefit many areas of life.

Identity Integration: Honoring your creative interests helps you feel more authentic and complete, reducing the psychological cost of suppressing important aspects of yourself.

Joy and Meaning: Creative expression can provide fulfillment and purpose that make other life challenges feel more manageable.

Social Connection: Creative communities offer relationships based on shared interests and mutual support rather than just professional networking.

Daily Integration

Today, do something creative for at least 15 minutes without justifying it as productive or practical. This might be doodling during a meeting, writing in a journal, singing along to music, cooking creatively, or any form of artistic expression that appeals to you.

Pay attention to how you feel before, during, and after engaging with creativity. Notice any guilt, resistance, or internal criticism that arises, and practice treating those thoughts with curiosity rather than immediately accepting them as truth.

Also consider how creativity might already show up in your life in ways you don't typically recognize—problem-solving at work, decorating your living space, choosing outfits, or planning social gatherings. Acknowledging existing creativity can help you feel more connected to your artistic nature.

Tomorrow's Preparation

As you interact with mirrors, photos, or any reflective surfaces today, notice your automatic thoughts about your physical appearance. Pay attention to your internal commentary about your body, face, or overall attractiveness. These observations will help us explore body image shadows and the impact of growing up with digital image manipulation technology.

Having cleared this conceptual space, you're ready to examine another area where authentic self-acceptance often gets compromised: your relationship with your physical body and appearance in an era of constant digital comparison and image manipulation.

Day 13: Body Image in the Filter Generation

Daily Check-In

Before looking in any mirrors or checking your appearance today, take a moment to notice how you feel about your body right now, in this moment, without any external feedback. What's your internal sense of comfort, appreciation, or criticism toward your physical self? How does that change when you imagine being seen or photographed by others?

You're probably familiar with the automatic habit of checking your appearance before video calls, adjusting poses for photos, or feeling disappointed when your real face doesn't match your filtered selfies. Maybe you've noticed yourself comparing your unfiltered morning reflection to the polished images you see online, or feeling confused about what you actually look like without digital enhancement.

Your generation has a unique relationship with body image because you came of age during the emergence of photo editing technology, social media, and beauty filters. This means your relationship with your physical appearance developed alongside digital tools that make image manipulation seem normal and expected. The result is often confusion between authentic self-acceptance and appearance optimization.

Growing Up with Photo Editing Technology

Previous generations formed their body image through mirrors, photographs, and in-person interactions—all of which showed them relatively accurate representations of their appearance. Your generation developed body image awareness while also learning to

106

use filters, editing apps, and image manipulation tools that became standard parts of social interaction.

This created what psychologists call "digital dysmorphia"— confusion about your actual appearance because you're accustomed to seeing edited versions of yourself and others. You might feel disappointed by your unfiltered reflection, not because you look bad, but because you look different from the digitally enhanced version you've become used to seeing.

Additionally, you've been exposed to thousands of edited images daily through social media, advertising, and entertainment media. Your brain learned to process these enhanced images as normal standards of appearance, making natural human features seem inadequate by comparison.

The psychological impact goes beyond vanity. When your daily visual environment consists primarily of digitally perfected images, your brain's reference point for normal human appearance becomes distorted. This can lead to body dysmorphia, eating disorders, and chronic dissatisfaction with perfectly healthy, attractive features.

Diet Culture and Body Shame Shadows

Your generation also grew up during the height of diet culture messaging, where bodies were treated as projects to be optimized rather than homes to be appreciated. The wellness industry emerged alongside social media, creating new forms of body shame disguised as health consciousness.

Wellness Culture Perfectionism: The pressure to have the optimal diet, exercise routine, sleep schedule, and supplement regimen can create anxiety about every aspect of physical self-care. Your body becomes another area where you need to perform perfection rather than simply exist comfortably.

Before and After Mentality: Social media created constant exposure to transformation stories and progress photos, reinforcing the idea that your current body is a temporary situation to be improved rather than an acceptable reality to be appreciated.

Productivity Body Shame: When productivity and optimization become primary values, your body's need for rest, pleasure, and varying energy levels can feel like failures rather than natural human characteristics.

Moral Food Categories: Diet culture attached moral value to food choices, making eating become a source of judgment and shame rather than nourishment and pleasure. You might feel guilty about enjoying "bad" foods or virtuous about eating "clean."

One person recognized their body image shadow: "I realized I never looked in mirrors anymore without automatically critiquing something—my skin, my weight, my hair, whatever. I was treating my body like a constant improvement project instead of appreciating it for carrying me through life. I couldn't remember the last time I looked at myself with neutral acceptance, let alone actual appreciation."

Exercise: Body Shadow Healing

This exercise helps you identify specific ways that digital culture and appearance pressures have affected your relationship with your physical self, and explore more accepting ways to relate to your body.

Step 1: The Body Image History Assessment

Write about how your relationship with your physical appearance has evolved over time:

- What did you think about your body and appearance as a young child?

- How did your body image change during adolescence and early social media exposure?

- When did you start using filters, editing photos, or comparing yourself to digital images?

- What messages did you receive about the importance of physical appearance?

- How has your body image affected your relationships, career choices, or social activities?

What patterns do you notice in when your body image became more critical or anxious?

How much of your appearance concerns are based on actual feedback versus internalized digital standards?

Step 2: The Digital Influence Analysis

Explore how digital technology has shaped your body image:

- How often do you use filters or editing on photos of yourself?

- What happens when you see unfiltered photos or unflattering images of yourself?

- How do you feel about your appearance in video calls versus photos versus mirrors?

- Which social media accounts or content consistently make you feel worse about your appearance?

- What beauty standards do you hold yourself to that might be based on digital manipulation?

How might constant exposure to edited images have affected your perception of normal human appearance?

What would change if you spent more time seeing unfiltered, natural human bodies?

Step 3: The Body Criticism Inventory

Write about the ways you habitually criticize or judge your physical appearance:

- What body parts or features do you consistently find fault with?

- What appearance-related thoughts run through your mind when you look in mirrors?

- How do you talk to yourself about your body when getting dressed or exercising?

- What physical characteristics do you try to hide or minimize?

- How much time do you spend thinking about changing your appearance?

Which body criticisms would you never say to a friend about their appearance?

How much mental and emotional energy do you spend on appearance concerns?

Step 4: The Body Appreciation Experiment

Write about aspects of your physical self that you could appreciate more:

- What does your body do for you beyond how it looks?

- What physical sensations or capabilities bring you joy or comfort?

- How has your body supported you through challenges or changes?

- What would it feel like to treat your body as a trusted companion rather than a project?

- How might your life change if you spent less energy criticizing your appearance?

What would it look like to approach your body with curiosity and appreciation rather than judgment?

How might body acceptance affect your relationships, career confidence, or social activities?

Reflection Questions

How has growing up with digital image manipulation affected your sense of what "normal" bodies look like?

What would change about your daily experience if you believed your body was acceptable as it is right now?

How do you distinguish between healthy self-care and appearance-focused self-improvement?

What would you focus your energy on if you weren't spending mental resources criticizing your appearance?

Radical Self-Acceptance Practices

Developing a healthier relationship with your body doesn't require loving every aspect of your appearance, but it does involve treating your physical self with basic respect and appreciation rather than constant criticism.

Functional Appreciation: Focus on what your body does rather than just how it looks. Appreciate your hands for creating things, your legs for carrying you places, your senses for bringing you information about the world.

Mirror Neutrality: Practice looking in mirrors with neutral observation rather than automatic criticism. Can you see yourself without immediately judging or trying to fix something?

Unfiltered Reality: Spend time with unfiltered images of yourself and others. Let your eyes adjust to natural human appearance without digital enhancement.

Body Diversity Exposure: Follow social media accounts that show diverse, unedited bodies. Retrain your brain to recognize the full spectrum of normal human appearance.

Comfort Over Appearance: Make choices based on physical comfort and well-being rather than only considering how things look. Wear clothes that feel good, eat foods that nourish you, move in ways that feel enjoyable.

Critical Voice Awareness: Notice when your internal voice becomes critical about appearance and practice responding with neutral or kind observations instead.

Working with Appearance Anxiety

If your body image significantly affects your daily life, relationships, or activities, consider that this might be more about anxiety and perfectionism than about your actual appearance. Most appearance concerns are psychological rather than physical issues.

Social Media Boundaries: Limit exposure to content that consistently triggers appearance comparison or inadequacy. Unfollow accounts that make you feel worse about yourself.

Reality Check: Ask trusted friends or family members for honest feedback about whether your appearance concerns match their perception of you.

Professional Support: If body image issues significantly impact your life, consider working with a therapist who specializes in body image and eating concerns.

Self-Compassion: Treat appearance concerns with the same kindness you'd show a friend struggling with similar issues. Body image anxiety is common and understandable given cultural pressures.

Daily Integration

Today, practice interacting with your reflection and photos without automatic criticism. When you catch yourself focusing on perceived flaws or imperfections, experiment with neutral observation or appreciation for what your body provides you.

Also pay attention to how appearance concerns affect your choices throughout the day. Are you avoiding activities, social interactions, or experiences because of body image anxiety? Notice these patterns without judgment, but consider whether appearance concerns are limiting your life in ways that don't serve you.

Try spending time in your body through movement, stretching, or physical activities that help you connect with how your body feels rather than just how it looks.

Tomorrow's Preparation

Tonight, gather all your notes from this week's exercises. Tomorrow you'll be integrating your discoveries from Days 8-13 into a comprehensive understanding of your shadow patterns and preparing for the transformation work that begins next week.

As these patterns become visible, you're ready to step back and see how all the shadow elements you've discovered this week connect to create a complete picture of your unconscious patterns and their impact on your daily life.

Day 14: Week 2 Integration: Recognizing Your Patterns

Daily Check-In

Take a moment to acknowledge the depth of self-exploration you've accomplished this week. You've examined climate anxiety, people-pleasing, perfectionism, suppressed anger, creative sacrifice, and body image concerns—all areas where many people spend their whole lives avoiding honest self-reflection. You're developing the kind of self-awareness that creates genuine possibilities for change and growth.

As you prepare to synthesize this week's discoveries, notice any impulses to minimize what you've learned or convince yourself that these patterns aren't really that significant. This minimization is often a protective response when you've uncovered patterns that feel overwhelming to address. Remember that awareness itself is the first step toward more conscious choices.

This week revealed the sophisticated ways your psyche has adapted to challenging cultural conditions. Each shadow pattern served a purpose—protecting you from disappointment, helping you navigate social pressure, managing anxiety about an uncertain future. Understanding this helps you approach these patterns with appreciation rather than judgment.

Understanding the Interconnections

The shadow patterns you explored this week aren't isolated behaviors—they're connected responses to the unique pressures your generation has faced. Climate anxiety might connect to perfectionism through shared themes about control and helplessness. People-pleasing might relate to anger suppression through avoidance of conflict. Body image concerns might link to creative suppression through patterns of self-criticism and inadequacy.

These connections matter because working with shadow patterns is most effective when you understand their underlying dynamics rather than just addressing surface behaviors. Your climate anxiety might not just be about environmental concerns—it might also be about feeling powerless in other areas of life. Your perfectionism might not just be about high standards—it might be about using achievement to manage uncertainty about the future.

Common Underlying Themes:

Control vs. Acceptance: Many millennial shadow patterns involve attempting to control uncontrollable situations or suppressing natural responses to circumstances beyond your influence.

Performance vs. Authenticity: The pressure to present optimized versions of yourself across multiple contexts can create internal splits between who you are and who you think you need to be.

Individual vs. Community: Messages about self-reliance and personal achievement can conflict with natural needs for support, connection, and interdependence.

Security vs. Growth: Economic uncertainty can create tension between prioritizing safety and pursuing fulfillment, often leading to suppression of natural expansion impulses.

Exercise: Pattern Synthesis Mandala

This exercise uses a visual format to help you see the relationships between different shadow patterns and identify your most significant themes for integration work.

Step 1: The Pattern Collection

Review your notes from Days 8-13 and identify the most significant patterns you discovered. For each day, write 2-3 key insights about yourself:

Day 8 (Climate/Future Anxiety): What did you learn about how uncertainty affects your daily choices and emotional state?

Day 9 (People-Pleasing): What patterns did you recognize in how you manage relationships and seek approval?

Day 10 (Perfectionism): What did you discover about achievement pressure and image management?

Day 11 (Suppressed Anger): How do conflict avoidance and indirect anger expression show up in your life?

Day 12 (Creative Sacrifice): What did you learn about the relationship between creativity and practical concerns?

Day 13 (Body Image): How do appearance concerns and digital comparison affect your self-relationship?

Step 2: The Connection Mapping

Create a visual representation of how these patterns connect. This could be a traditional mandala, a web diagram, or any visual format that appeals to you. Include:

- Your main shadow patterns from each day
- Lines or connections between patterns that seem related
- Central themes that appear across multiple areas
- Colors or symbols that represent different emotional qualities

What connections surprise you?

Which patterns seem most fundamental or influential in your life?

What themes appear across multiple shadow areas?

Step 3: The Core Shadow Theme Identification

Based on your pattern mapping, write 1-2 sentences that capture your most central shadow themes. These should be broad enough to encompass multiple patterns but specific enough to guide integration work.

Examples might include:

- "I've learned to suppress my authentic needs and responses in order to maintain control and avoid disappointing others, but this creates internal pressure and resentment."

- "I use perfectionism and people-pleasing to manage anxiety about not being good enough, but this prevents me from experiencing genuine acceptance and connection."

What would you say is your core shadow theme?

How does this theme create both protection and limitation in your life?

Step 4: The Integration Priority Setting

Looking at your complete pattern map, choose 1-2 areas where you feel most ready to begin integration work. Consider:

- Which patterns feel most limiting or costly in your daily life?

- Where do you have the most energy and motivation for change?

- Which areas have the most support available (relationships, resources, etc.)?

- What feels most accessible as a starting point without overwhelming yourself?

Which shadow patterns feel most ready for conscious integration work?

What would be possible in your life if you could work with these patterns more consciously?

Reflection Questions

What has been the most surprising discovery about yourself over these past two weeks?

How do your shadow patterns both protect and limit you?

What connections do you see between your personal patterns and broader generational challenges?

How has your understanding of "self-improvement" changed through this shadow work process?

Preparing for Integration Work

Next week begins the active integration phase of this shadow work process. Integration doesn't mean eliminating shadow patterns or becoming a different person. It means developing conscious relationships with all aspects of your personality so you can choose how to express them rather than being controlled by unconscious dynamics.

Integration Principles:

Acceptance Before Change: You can't successfully modify patterns you haven't fully accepted as part of yourself. Integration starts with acknowledging that these patterns developed for good reasons.

Conscious Choice: The goal is increasing your range of responses rather than eliminating certain behaviors. Sometimes people-pleasing is appropriate; sometimes directness is needed. Integration gives you options.

Gradual Process: Shadow integration happens slowly through consistent small choices rather than dramatic personality overhauls. Expect the work to unfold over months and years, not days.

Support and Community: This work is easier with support from friends, family, or professionals who understand growth processes. Consider what support resources you might need.

Self-Compassion: Treat yourself with the same kindness you'd show a good friend doing this work. Shadow integration involves vulnerability and mistakes—both are normal parts of the process.

Daily Integration

Today, spend time with your pattern map or visual representation, adding to it as new insights arise. Consider sharing appropriate parts of your discoveries with trusted people in your life who might offer supportive perspective or encouragement.

Practice holding your shadow patterns with curiosity rather than judgment. These patterns developed as intelligent adaptations to challenging circumstances. They deserve appreciation for how they've served you, even if they're ready for modification.

Begin considering what support or resources might help you as you move into more active integration work. This might include friends who understand personal growth, books or podcasts about relevant topics, or professional support if certain patterns feel too challenging to address alone.

Tomorrow's Preparation

As you begin Week 3, you'll start working more directly with shadow integration techniques. Prepare by setting an intention for what you'd like to develop or change about your relationship with your shadow patterns. What would feel meaningful to accomplish over the next week?

With this scaffolding erected, you're ready to move beyond recognition and analysis into active integration work, where you'll develop practical skills for working with your shadow patterns consciously in daily life.

Day 15: Active Dialogue with Your Shadow Self

Daily Check-In

Take a moment to imagine having a conversation with the parts of yourself that you usually try to ignore or suppress. What would your inner perfectionist want to tell you? What might your people-pleasing self need you to understand? What would your suppressed anger or hidden creative impulses want to express? Notice whether the idea of listening to these parts feels curious, scary, or something in between.

You've probably experienced moments when different aspects of your personality seem to be in conflict with each other. Maybe part of you wants to take career risks while another part demands security. Perhaps you feel torn between expressing authentic opinions and maintaining social harmony. These internal conflicts often represent conversations between your conscious self and your shadow aspects that have been trying to get your attention.

Most people try to resolve these conflicts by choosing one side and suppressing the other. But shadow work suggests a different approach: instead of eliminating the uncomfortable parts, you can learn to dialogue with them directly. This doesn't mean indulging every impulse, but it does mean understanding what your shadow aspects are trying to provide or protect before making decisions about how to respond.

Advanced Shadow Work Techniques

Moving beyond recognition into active integration requires developing skills for communicating with unconscious parts of yourself. These techniques come from various psychological traditions but share the common goal of making unconscious patterns conscious so you can work with them intentionally.

Active Imagination: This involves creating intentional conversations with different aspects of your personality, treating them as distinct voices or characters that have their own perspectives and needs. Rather than judging these parts, you approach them with curiosity about what they're trying to accomplish.

Internal Family Systems: This approach recognizes that everyone contains multiple sub-personalities or "parts" that developed at different times and for different purposes. Shadow work becomes about understanding how these parts interact and finding ways for them to work together rather than against each other.

Shadow Dialogue: This technique involves writing conversations between your conscious self and specific shadow aspects, allowing each part to express its concerns, fears, and desires without interruption or judgment.

Body-Based Awareness: Since shadow aspects often express themselves through physical sensations, tension, or energy changes, learning to notice and dialogue with these bodily experiences can provide access to unconscious patterns.

Creating Internal Dialogue Practices

The key to effective shadow dialogue is approaching your unconscious aspects with the same respect and curiosity you'd show an actual person whose perspective you wanted to understand. This means temporarily suspending judgment and allowing parts of yourself to explain their point of view fully before responding.

Setting Up Dialogues: Choose a quiet space where you won't be interrupted and have something to write with. Begin by addressing a specific shadow aspect directly, as if it were another person sitting across from you. Ask open-ended questions and write down whatever responses arise, even if they seem silly or unexpected.

Common Dialogue Starters:

- "What are you trying to protect me from?"

- "What do you need me to understand about your perspective?"

- "When did you first start trying to help me this way?"

- "What are you afraid would happen if you stopped doing this?"

- "What would you like from me going forward?"

Maintaining Curiosity: The most important element is genuine curiosity rather than trying to talk your shadow aspects out of their concerns. Even when their methods feel problematic, there's usually something valuable they're trying to provide.

One person described their first shadow dialogue experience: "I was amazed when I started writing from my perfectionist part's perspective. I expected it to just be critical and demanding, but it was actually scared and trying to protect me from the shame of making mistakes. Once I understood that, I could work with it more compassively instead of just fighting against it."

Exercise: Shadow Conversation Technique

This exercise guides you through creating a structured dialogue with one specific shadow aspect, helping you understand its perspective and find ways to work together more consciously.

Step 1: Shadow Aspect Selection

Choose one shadow pattern that you'd like to understand better. This might be:

- Your inner perfectionist

- Your people-pleasing tendencies

- Your conflict-avoidant part

- Your inner critic

- Your creative resistance

- Your relationship patterns

Which shadow aspect feels most prominent or challenging in your current life?

What would be helpful to understand about this part of yourself?

Step 2: Setting the Dialogue Scene

Find a quiet space and imagine this shadow aspect as a distinct entity sitting across from you. You might visualize it as another version of yourself, an abstract energy, or even a metaphorical character. The important thing is treating it as having its own perspective that deserves to be heard.

Begin by introducing yourself and explaining your intention to understand this part better. You might say something like: "I've noticed that you've been working hard to help me in certain situations, and I'd like to understand your perspective better."

Step 3: The Conversation Process

Write out a conversation, alternating between your conscious voice and the shadow aspect's voice. Start with open-ended questions and let the dialogue develop naturally. Don't worry if the responses seem to come from your imagination—the goal is accessing unconscious perspectives, not literal communication with another entity.

Sample dialogue structure:

You: "What are you most concerned about in my life right now?"

Shadow Aspect: [Write whatever response arises, even if it surprises you]

You: "Can you help me understand when you first started trying to help me this way?"

Shadow Aspect: [Allow the response to emerge without editing]

Continue for 15-20 minutes, asking follow-up questions based on what emerges.

Step 4: Integration Planning

After the dialogue, write about what you learned and how you might work with this shadow aspect more consciously:

What did this part reveal about its motivations or concerns?

How might you honor what it's trying to provide while addressing any problematic aspects?

What would collaboration with this shadow aspect look like instead of internal conflict?

Reflection Questions

What surprised you most about your shadow dialogue experience?

How does this part of yourself show both protective and limiting qualities?

What would change if you treated this shadow aspect as an ally with valuable information rather than an enemy to defeat?

How might internal dialogue become a regular practice for better self-understanding?

Accessing Shadow Wisdom

One of the most surprising discoveries in shadow work is that the parts of yourself you've been avoiding often contain valuable wisdom and capabilities. Your perfectionist part might have high standards that could be channeled into meaningful projects. Your people-pleasing tendencies might reflect genuine empathy and social intelligence. Your suppressed anger might contain important information about boundary violations.

The Gifts in Shadow Patterns:

Perfectionism often contains valuable discernment, aesthetic sense, and commitment to quality. The challenge is learning when to apply these gifts rather than using them compulsively.

People-Pleasing frequently reflects genuine care for others, emotional intelligence, and collaborative skills. The work involves maintaining these qualities while also honoring your own needs.

Conflict Avoidance might contain wisdom about timing, diplomacy, and the value of harmony. The integration involves learning when peace-keeping serves relationships and when it prevents necessary conversations.

Achievement Drive often represents genuine passion, capability, and desire to contribute meaningfully. The shadow aspect appears when achievement becomes compulsive rather than flowing from authentic interests.

Control Tendencies frequently contain valuable planning skills, responsibility, and care for outcomes. The problematic element emerges when the need for control becomes rigid or extends to uncontrollable situations.

Working with Resistance

Your shadow aspects might initially be suspicious of dialogue attempts, especially if you've been trying to eliminate or ignore them for years. This resistance is normal and actually shows that these parts take their protective role seriously.

Common Forms of Resistance:

- Feeling silly or self-conscious about talking to yourself

- Getting responses that seem too simple or obvious

- Internal criticism about the dialogue process

- Difficulty accessing responses from shadow aspects

125

- Feeling like you're making everything up

Working with Resistance:

- Acknowledge that resistance makes sense given how you've related to these parts previously

- Start with shorter dialogues and build comfort gradually

- Remember that imagination and unconscious wisdom often overlap—trust the process even if responses seem to come from your creative mind

- Practice self-compassion about feeling awkward with new psychological techniques

Daily Integration

Today, experiment with brief internal check-ins with different parts of yourself throughout the day. Instead of automatically suppressing uncomfortable feelings or impulses, try asking them what they're responding to or what they need you to know.

This doesn't mean acting on every impulse, but it does mean gathering more information before making decisions. You might discover that your procrastination is trying to protect you from overwhelming pressure, or that your social anxiety contains valuable information about certain environments.

Practice treating these internal responses as information rather than commands. You can thank parts of yourself for their input while still choosing how to respond based on your current values and circumstances.

Tomorrow's Preparation

As you go through today, notice moments when you feel powerless, small, or like you're not enough to handle what's in front of you. Also pay attention to times when you feel genuinely confident and capable. These observations will help us explore how to reclaim authentic personal power tomorrow.

Now that you've explored this territory, you're ready to discover how shadow integration can actually increase your sense of personal power and authentic confidence rather than just making you more self-aware.

Day 16: Reclaiming Your Authentic Power

Daily Check-In

Before thinking about your goals, challenges, or anyone else's expectations, take a moment to connect with your natural sense of personal power. What does it feel like when you're operating from genuine confidence rather than trying to prove something? When have you felt most like yourself while also feeling capable and strong? Notice whether accessing this feeling comes easily or if you have to search for it.

You've probably noticed that some situations or people seem to drain your energy and make you feel smaller, while others help you feel more capable and alive. Maybe you've experienced moments of feeling truly powerful—not in a dominating way, but in a grounded, authentic way where you knew you could handle whatever came up. Then other times, you might feel like you're performing competence while internally feeling inadequate or overwhelmed.

Many millennials have complicated relationships with personal power because you came of age during a time when traditional power structures were being questioned while new forms of empowerment weren't clearly established. This can create confusion about what healthy power looks like and how to access it authentically.

Shadow as Source of Personal Strength

One of the biggest misconceptions about shadow work is that it's only about addressing problematic patterns. In reality, your shadow often contains some of your greatest sources of power and strength— qualities that went underground not because they were bad, but because they didn't fit certain social expectations or circumstances.

128

Your shadow might contain your natural leadership abilities that were suppressed because you learned to be humble. It might hold your fierce protective instincts that were discouraged because you were taught to be nice. Your competitive drive might be hiding because you learned that winning made others feel bad. Your passionate intensity might be buried because you were told you were "too much."

Common Sources of Shadow Power:

Suppressed Assertiveness: Your ability to advocate for yourself, set boundaries, and express disagreement might have gone underground if it conflicted with being likeable or accommodating. But this assertiveness is often crucial for healthy relationships and career success.

Hidden Confidence: Your natural self-assurance might be suppressed behind humble or self-deprecating presentation. Accessing this confidence doesn't mean becoming arrogant—it means owning your capabilities without apology.

Buried Ambition: Your genuine desire for achievement, recognition, or success might feel shameful if you were taught that ambition is selfish. But healthy ambition can fuel meaningful contribution and personal growth.

Disguised Intensity: Your passionate, emotionally expressive nature might be toned down to fit social expectations about being calm and reasonable. But this intensity often contains your greatest creativity and authentic engagement.

Underground Wisdom: Your intuitive knowledge about people, situations, or yourself might be dismissed if you learned to prioritize rational analysis over gut instincts. But this wisdom is often more accurate than logical reasoning alone.

Millennial Empowerment Strategies

Your generation faces unique challenges in accessing authentic power because many traditional sources of empowerment—stable career paths, predictable economic conditions, established social hierarchies—are no longer reliable. This requires developing new approaches to personal power that work within current realities.

Internal vs. External Power: Previous generations could often rely on external sources of power—job titles, institutional authority, financial security—to feel capable and confident. Millennials often need to develop internal sources of power that don't depend on external validation or circumstances.

Collaborative vs. Competitive Power: Your generation tends to value collaboration and mutual support over pure competition. This requires learning to be powerful in ways that lift others up rather than putting them down.

Authentic vs. Performed Power: Social media culture created pressure to perform confidence and success. Authentic power involves feeling genuinely capable even when your external circumstances aren't perfect or when others can't see your strength.

Flexible vs. Rigid Power: Economic and social uncertainty requires power that can adapt to changing circumstances rather than depending on maintaining specific conditions or roles.

One person described reclaiming their power: "I realized I'd been trying to be powerful by being perfect—never making mistakes, always having the right answer, controlling every outcome. But that just made me anxious and exhausted. Real power for me came from accepting that I could handle whatever happened, even if I didn't know how to prevent problems from arising."

Exercise: Power Reclamation Ritual

This exercise helps you identify sources of authentic power within your shadow and create intentions for accessing these qualities more consciously in daily life.

Step 1: Power History Assessment

Write about your relationship with personal power throughout different life stages:

- When did you feel most naturally powerful as a child or teenager?

- What qualities or abilities made you feel confident and capable?

- When did you start questioning or suppressing these powerful aspects of yourself?

- What messages did you receive about what makes someone legitimately powerful?

- How has your relationship with power changed since entering adulthood?

Which sources of power felt most natural and authentic to you originally?

When did you learn to hide or minimize your power, and why?

Step 2: Shadow Power Identification

Explore aspects of your personality that might contain untapped power:

- What qualities do you admire in others that you might also possess but not express?

- When do people describe you as strong, capable, or impressive in ways that surprise you?

- What aspects of yourself do you tone down or hide in social situations?

- What would you be like if you weren't concerned about being too much, too intense, or too ambitious?

- What natural talents or instincts do you dismiss as not important enough?

Which suppressed qualities might actually be sources of authentic power?

How might these hidden strengths serve you if they were expressed more consciously?

Step 3: The Power Reclamation Visualization

Find a quiet space and spend 10-15 minutes in a guided visualization:

Close your eyes and imagine yourself operating from complete authentic power—not dominating others, but fully owning your capabilities, wisdom, and strength. See yourself moving through your typical day with this energy. How do you walk, speak, and make decisions? How do you handle challenges or conflicts? How do others respond to your authentic power?

What did you notice about yourself when operating from authentic power?

How did this feel different from trying to prove your competence or manage others' perceptions?

Step 4: Power Integration Planning

Choose 2-3 specific ways you could begin expressing more authentic power in your daily life:

- Situations where you could speak up more confidently

- Decisions where you could trust your instincts more fully

- Relationships where you could set firmer boundaries

- Professional contexts where you could own your expertise more directly

- Creative or personal projects where you could take up more space

What would be the first small step toward expressing more authentic power in each area?

What support or resources would help you maintain this empowered energy?

Reflection Questions

How do you distinguish between authentic power and trying to control or dominate others?

What would change about your daily experience if you fully believed in your own capabilities?

How might your relationships improve if you brought more of your authentic power to them?

What would you pursue or create if you felt genuinely powerful rather than needing to prove yourself?

Setting Empowered Intentions

Moving from recognition to action requires setting intentions that align with your authentic sources of power rather than trying to become someone else's version of powerful. Empowered intentions feel energizing and sustainable because they're based on your actual strengths and values rather than external expectations.

Characteristics of Empowered Intentions:

Intrinsically Motivated: They come from your genuine interests and values rather than trying to meet others' expectations or prove your worth.

Strength-Based: They utilize your natural capabilities and talents rather than trying to compensate for perceived weaknesses.

Growth-Oriented: They challenge you to expand while still feeling achievable with your current resources and support systems.

Authentic to Your Style: They fit your personality and preferred ways of operating rather than copying someone else's approach to success.

Flexible in Method: They focus on outcomes you want to create while staying open to different paths for achieving them.

Working with Power Anxiety

Many people, especially those who grew up as sensitive or thoughtful children, develop anxiety about their own power. You might worry about becoming arrogant, hurting others, or losing the approval that came from being humble and accommodating.

Common Power Fears:

- Being seen as arrogant or self-important

- Making others feel threatened or inadequate

- Losing relationships if you become more confident

- Making mistakes when others are depending on your strength

- Having your power be temporary or based on false confidence

Addressing Power Anxiety:

- Remember that authentic power usually makes others feel more capable, not less

- Practice expressing power in small, safe situations to build confidence

- Distinguish between healthy confidence and arrogance—one lifts others up, the other puts them down

- Accept that some people might be uncomfortable with your growth, and that's their process to work through

- Trust that relationships based on your small, accommodating self weren't serving either person fully

Daily Integration

Today, experiment with taking up slightly more space—literally and figuratively. This might mean speaking up more in conversations, expressing opinions more confidently, or simply walking and sitting with more presence and groundedness.

Pay attention to moments when you automatically make yourself smaller or defer to others when you actually have valuable insights or capabilities to offer. Practice offering your perspective even when you're not sure how it will be received.

Notice the difference between performing confidence and feeling genuinely powerful. Performed confidence often feels effortful and anxiety-provoking. Authentic power usually feels more relaxed and grounded, even when you're taking risks or handling challenges.

Tomorrow's Preparation

As you move through today, pay attention to areas where you consistently undermine your own success or avoid opportunities that you're actually qualified for. Notice any patterns of procrastination, self-doubt, or giving up when things get challenging. These observations will help us explore self-sabotage patterns tomorrow.

From this place of knowing, you're ready to examine the ways that reclaimed power can be undermined by unconscious self-sabotage patterns, and learn to recognize these patterns before they derail your authentic empowerment.

Day 17: Breaking Millennial Self-Sabotage Cycles

Daily Check-In

Think about a recent opportunity that you were genuinely excited about but somehow didn't follow through on, or a goal you set with enthusiasm that faded when you actually needed to take action. What happened between your initial excitement and your eventual avoidance? Can you remember the specific thoughts, feelings, or circumstances that led to backing down or giving up?

You've probably noticed patterns where you get in your own way just when things are starting to work out. Maybe you procrastinate on projects you care about, or you find reasons why opportunities aren't quite right for you, or you create conflicts in relationships that are going well. These behaviors often feel confusing and frustrating because they seem to work against your conscious desires.

Self-sabotage isn't a character flaw or evidence of laziness—it's usually your psyche's attempt to protect you from perceived dangers that come with success, visibility, or change. Understanding what your self-sabotage patterns are trying to protect you from is the first step toward working with them more consciously.

Understanding Self-Defeating Patterns

Self-sabotage typically happens when unconscious parts of your mind perceive success as threatening in some way. These threats might include fear of increased responsibility, anxiety about sustaining success, worry about outgrowing important relationships, or deep beliefs about not deserving good things.

For millennials, self-sabotage patterns often develop from the intersection of high expectations and uncertain conditions. You were encouraged to achieve at high levels while facing economic instability, competitive job markets, and social pressures that previous generations didn't experience. This can create internal conflicts where success feels both necessary and dangerous.

Common Millennial Self-Sabotage Patterns:

Perfectionism Paralysis: Setting standards so high that you can't start or complete projects because they won't be perfect. This protects you from judgment while preventing you from learning through practice and feedback.

Success Anxiety: Feeling increasingly uncomfortable as opportunities expand or recognition grows. The anxiety of maintaining success can feel worse than the disappointment of not trying.

Impostor Syndrome Acting Out: Unconsciously creating evidence that you don't belong in successful roles by making mistakes, avoiding networking, or downplaying achievements.

Relationship Sacrifice: Prioritizing others' comfort over your own growth, sometimes sabotaging opportunities to avoid making others feel left behind or threatened.

Financial Self-Sabotage: Overspending, avoiding financial planning, or making poor money decisions that prevent you from building security or funding your goals.

One person recognized their pattern: "I realized I had a habit of creating chaos whenever life was going too smoothly. If work was good, I'd create relationship drama. If my relationship was stable, I'd make impulsive career decisions. It was like I couldn't handle things being consistently good, so I'd unconsciously create problems to bring myself back to a familiar level of struggle."

Imposter Syndrome and Success Fear

Imposter syndrome is particularly common among millennials because you entered competitive environments where external metrics of success became primary measures of worth. When your value feels tied to achievements rather than inherent human worth, success can feel precarious and anxiety-provoking.

The Imposter Syndrome Cycle:

1. You achieve something or receive recognition

2. Instead of feeling proud, you worry that you fooled people or got lucky

3. You work harder to prove you deserve the success, often leading to burnout

4. You avoid situations that might expose your "inadequacy"

5. This avoidance prevents further growth and reinforces feelings of being a fraud

How Success Fear Creates Self-Sabotage:

- **Visibility Anxiety**: Success makes you more visible, which can trigger fears about criticism, judgment, or having your flaws exposed

- **Responsibility Pressure**: Achievement often comes with increased expectations and responsibilities that can feel overwhelming

- **Relationship Concerns**: Success might change your relationships or make others feel threatened

- **Sustainability Worries**: You might doubt your ability to maintain success, so failing early feels safer than failing later

- **Identity Conflicts**: Success might conflict with how you see yourself or how others see you

Exercise: Sabotage Pattern Interruption

This exercise helps you identify your specific self-sabotage patterns and develop strategies for recognizing and interrupting them before they derail your progress.

Step 1: Self-Sabotage Pattern Identification

Think about the last few times you got in your own way or failed to follow through on something important. For each situation, write about:

- What you were trying to achieve or the opportunity you had

- What happened to prevent you from following through

- The thoughts, feelings, or circumstances that led to giving up

- What you told yourself about why it didn't work out

- How you felt afterward about the missed opportunity

What patterns do you notice in how you sabotage yourself?

Which types of success or visibility seem to trigger self-sabotage most?

Step 2: The Fear Investigation

For each self-sabotage pattern you identified, explore what you might have been unconsciously trying to avoid:

- What could have gone wrong if you had succeeded?

- What responsibilities or pressures would success have created?

- How might success have changed your relationships or identity?

- What beliefs do you have about people who achieve what you want?

- What familiar struggles would you have had to give up if things worked out?

What is your self-sabotage trying to protect you from?

How might these concerns be both valid and limiting?

Step 3: The Success Visualization Challenge

Choose one current goal or opportunity where you notice self-sabotage tendencies. Spend 10 minutes visualizing complete success in this area, including:

- What achievement would look like

- How you would feel about yourself

- How others would respond to your success

- What your daily life would be like

- What new challenges or responsibilities would arise

Pay attention to any anxiety, resistance, or discomfort that comes up during this visualization.

What felt scary or uncomfortable about imagining complete success?

Which aspects of success feel genuinely exciting versus which feel threatening?

Step 4: The Pattern Interruption Strategy

For your main self-sabotage pattern, develop a specific strategy for interrupting it when it begins:

- What are the early warning signs that you're starting to sabotage yourself?

- What could you do differently when you notice these warning signs?

- What supportive self-talk could replace the usual self-sabotage thoughts?

- Who could you reach out to for encouragement when you feel like giving up?

- What small action could you take to maintain momentum even when motivation decreases?

What would be most helpful to remember when you're tempted to sabotage your progress?

Reflection Questions

How do your self-sabotage patterns both protect and limit you?

What would change about your life if you could sustain success without creating problems?

How might your fears about success be based on outdated beliefs rather than current realities?

What kind of support would help you feel safer about achieving your goals?

Creating Success Support Systems

One of the most effective ways to address self-sabotage is creating support systems that help you navigate success rather than avoiding it. This involves both internal support (changing your relationship with success) and external support (people and resources that help you handle achievement).

Internal Support Systems:

Redefining Success: Instead of defining success as achieving specific external outcomes, consider including values like authenticity, growth, contribution, and well-being in your success criteria.

Process Focus: Celebrate effort, learning, and progress rather than only acknowledging final achievements. This makes success less anxiety-provoking because it's not dependent on perfect outcomes.

Identity Flexibility: Practice seeing yourself as someone who can grow and change rather than someone with fixed limitations. Success doesn't have to threaten your core identity if that identity includes capacity for expansion.

Self-Compassion: Treat yourself with the same kindness during success as during struggle. Many people are more comfortable with self-criticism than self-appreciation.

External Support Systems:

Success Peers: Connect with others who are pursuing similar goals and can normalize the challenges of growth and achievement.

Mentorship: Find people who have achieved what you want and can help you navigate the practical and emotional aspects of success.

Accountability: Work with friends, coaches, or colleagues who can help you stay committed to your goals when motivation fluctuates.

Professional Support: Consider therapy or coaching if self-sabotage patterns are significantly impacting your life or if they seem connected to deeper emotional issues.

Working with Impostor Syndrome

Addressing impostor syndrome involves changing your relationship with competence and achievement rather than trying to feel completely confident all the time. Most successful people experience some degree of impostor syndrome—it's often a sign that you're pushing beyond your comfort zone.

Practical Strategies:

Evidence Collection: Keep track of positive feedback, achievements, and growth rather than dismissing these as flukes or luck.

Skill Inventory: Regularly assess your actual capabilities and knowledge rather than focusing on what you don't know yet.

Learning Orientation: Treat challenges as opportunities to develop rather than tests of your worth or competence.

Competence vs. Perfection: Accept that you can be competent without knowing everything or never making mistakes.

External Validation Balance: Value others' feedback without making it the primary source of your self-worth.

Daily Integration

Today, practice catching self-sabotage thoughts as they arise and getting curious about what they're trying to protect you from. When you notice yourself procrastinating, making excuses, or avoiding opportunities, pause and ask what you're afraid might happen if you succeeded.

Also experiment with taking small actions toward your goals even when motivation is low or anxiety is high. Self-sabotage often works by convincing you to wait until you feel more confident or prepared. Practice moving forward with imperfect confidence and seeing what happens.

Pay attention to how you talk to yourself about your achievements and capabilities. Practice acknowledging your competence and progress without immediately minimizing or qualifying these recognitions.

Tomorrow's Preparation

As you interact with others today, notice how you communicate your needs, boundaries, and authentic perspectives in relationships. Pay attention to when you're direct and honest versus when you edit yourself or avoid difficult conversations. These observations will help us explore conscious communication in relationships tomorrow.

With this foundation created, you're ready to explore how the self-awareness and personal power you've been developing can improve your relationships through more conscious, authentic communication.

Day 18: Conscious Communication in Modern Relationships

Daily Check-In

Before engaging in any conversations today, take a moment to notice your current emotional state and what you genuinely need from your interactions with others. Are you seeking connection, support, stimulation, or something else? How often do you check in with your authentic needs versus automatically focusing on managing others' experiences or reactions?

You've probably noticed that some conversations leave you feeling energized and understood, while others drain your energy or create confusion even when they seem pleasant on the surface. Maybe you've found yourself saying yes when you meant no, or avoiding important topics because you're not sure how to bring them up without creating conflict. These patterns often reflect unconscious shadow dynamics playing out in your relationships.

Conscious communication isn't about becoming a perfect communicator or always knowing the right thing to say. It's about bringing more awareness to how your shadow patterns affect your relationships, and learning to express your authentic self while remaining responsive to others' needs and boundaries.

Projection in Dating and Partnerships

One of the most common ways shadow patterns affect relationships is through projection—unconsciously seeing your own suppressed traits in your partner and reacting to them as if they belong entirely to the other person. This creates relationship conflicts that are actually about internal conflicts you haven't resolved.

145

For example, if you've suppressed your own neediness, you might become irritated when your partner asks for support, seeing them as too dependent rather than recognizing your own discomfort with vulnerability. If you've hidden your competitive nature, you might criticize your partner for being too ambitious while secretly envying their confidence.

Common Relationship Projections:

The Responsibility Projection: If you've learned to be overly responsible, you might attract partners who seem carefree or irresponsible, then feel resentful about carrying all the practical burdens. The shadow work involves recognizing your own need to relax and be cared for sometimes.

The Emotional Projection: If you've suppressed your emotional intensity, you might be drawn to dramatic partners, then feel exhausted by their expressiveness. Integration involves acknowledging and expressing your own full emotional range.

The Control Projection: If you've hidden your need for control, you might criticize partners for being controlling while ignoring your own subtle ways of managing situations and relationships.

The Success Projection: If you've suppressed your ambition, you might either attract highly driven partners (then resent their focus on achievement) or partners who lack direction (then feel frustrated by their lack of motivation).

One person recognized their projection pattern: "I kept dating people who seemed super independent and then feeling hurt when they didn't seem to need me enough. I realized I was projecting my own fear of neediness onto them. I was attracted to their independence because I'd suppressed that quality in myself, but then I felt rejected when they actually behaved independently."

Exercise: Relationship Shadow Cleanup

This exercise helps you identify specific ways your shadow patterns might be affecting your relationships and develop more conscious approaches to communication and connection.

Step 1: Relationship Pattern Analysis

Think about your last few significant relationships (romantic, friendship, or family) and identify recurring patterns:

- What types of people do you consistently find attractive or drawn to?

- What behaviors in others tend to trigger strong reactions in you?

- What relationship conflicts keep showing up with different people?

- What do you tend to criticize or try to change about partners or close friends?

- What aspects of relationships do you avoid or feel uncomfortable with?

Which relationship patterns seem to follow you regardless of who you're with?

What might these patterns reveal about your own shadow aspects?

Step 2: The Projection Investigation

For each relationship trigger you identified, explore how it might connect to your own shadow:

- What quality in others bothers you most, and how might you also have this quality?

- What do you expect or need from others that you have difficulty providing for yourself?

- What aspects of your personality do you try to hide or manage in relationships?

- How do you hope others will see you, and what are you afraid they'll discover?

Which external relationship problems might actually be internal conflicts being acted out?

How might your judgments of others reflect parts of yourself you haven't accepted?

Step 3: The Authentic Communication Assessment

Evaluate your current communication patterns in close relationships:

- What do you tend to avoid discussing, even with people you trust?

- When do you edit your responses or hide your authentic reactions?

- How do you typically handle disagreement or conflict?

- What do you wish people understood about you that you haven't directly communicated?

- How often do you ask for what you need versus hoping others will guess?

Where do you feel most and least authentic in your communication?

What prevents you from being more direct and honest in relationships?

Step 4: Conscious Communication Practice Planning

Choose one relationship where you could practice more conscious communication:

- What authentic aspect of yourself could you share more openly?

- What conversation have you been avoiding that might strengthen the relationship?

- What boundary do you need to set or request could you make more directly?

- How could you take more responsibility for your own emotional needs in this relationship?

What would be a small first step toward more authentic communication in this relationship?

Reflection Questions

How do your shadow patterns both protect and complicate your relationships?

What would change about your relationships if you expressed your authentic needs more directly?

How might some of your relationship conflicts be opportunities for shadow integration?

What kind of support would help you feel safer about being more authentic in relationships?

Healthy Communication Skills

Developing conscious communication skills involves learning to express yourself authentically while remaining emotionally available to others. This balance requires ongoing practice and self-awareness rather than perfect technique.

Owning Your Experience: Use "I" statements to describe your experience rather than making assumptions about others' intentions or character. "I felt hurt when..." rather than "You never..." or "You always..."

Direct Requests: Ask clearly for what you need rather than hoping others will guess or feeling resentful when they don't. Many relationship problems come from indirect communication that creates confusion.

Emotional Responsibility: Take responsibility for your emotional reactions while still sharing them appropriately. You can feel hurt by someone's behavior without making them responsible for managing your feelings.

Conflict as Information: View disagreements as opportunities to understand each other better rather than threats to the relationship. Most conflicts contain valuable information about both people's needs and values.

Timing and Setting: Choose appropriate times and places for important conversations. Emotional topics are easier to navigate when both people feel safe and have adequate time.

Taking Responsibility Without Blame

One of the most challenging aspects of conscious communication is learning to take responsibility for your part in relationship dynamics without taking on inappropriate blame or making others responsible for your growth.

Healthy Responsibility:

- Acknowledging how your behavior affects others
- Recognizing your role in relationship patterns
- Taking ownership of your emotional reactions
- Making changes in your communication when needed
- Apologizing for specific actions when appropriate

Inappropriate Responsibility:

- Taking on blame for others' choices or reactions
- Managing others' emotions to avoid your own discomfort

- Accepting treatment that violates your boundaries
- Changing yourself to avoid any relationship conflict
- Apologizing for having needs or feelings

Avoiding Blame:

- Focusing on specific behaviors rather than character judgments
- Staying curious about others' perspectives rather than assuming you know their motivations
- Acknowledging the difference between impact and intention
- Taking breaks from difficult conversations when emotions are too high
- Seeking to understand rather than to be right

Working with Communication Anxiety

Many people feel anxious about authentic communication because it involves vulnerability and the risk of rejection or conflict. These fears often make sense given past experiences, but they can prevent the deeper connections that come through honest interaction.

Common Communication Fears:

- Being rejected if people see your authentic personality
- Creating conflict by expressing disagreement or needs
- Being seen as too demanding, sensitive, or difficult
- Hurting others by setting boundaries or being honest
- Not knowing how to handle others' emotional reactions

Building Communication Confidence:

- Start with lower-stakes relationships and situations

- Practice expressing minor preferences before addressing major issues

- Notice that most people appreciate honesty more than perfect agreeability

- Accept that some discomfort is normal when developing new relationship skills

- Find supportive people who encourage your authentic expression

Daily Integration

Today, experiment with expressing one authentic aspect of yourself that you usually keep private in a relationship conversation. This might be sharing a genuine preference, expressing a feeling you normally hide, or asking directly for something you need.

Pay attention to moments when you automatically edit your responses or avoid topics that feel vulnerable. Get curious about what you're trying to protect or avoid, and consider whether these protective strategies are still necessary.

Also practice listening for the underlying needs or concerns beneath what others are saying, rather than just responding to their words. This deeper listening often helps conversations become more authentic and connected.

Tomorrow's Preparation

As you go through your workday, pay attention to moments when you feel most and least like yourself in professional contexts. Notice when your work aligns with your values versus when it feels like pure obligation or performance. These observations will help us explore career authenticity tomorrow.

These ideas naturally lead us to examine how the communication and authenticity skills you're developing can be applied to your professional life, creating more alignment between who you are and how you work.

Day 19: Career Authenticity Beyond Hustle Culture

Daily Check-In

Before checking email or thinking about your work tasks, pause and notice how you feel when you imagine your ideal workday. What would you be doing? How would you feel during and after work? How does that compare to your current relationship with your career? Is there excitement, resignation, or something in between when you think about your professional life?

You've probably felt pressure to be passionate about your career while also being practical about financial security. Maybe you've tried to follow advice about finding your purpose while dealing with student loans, competitive job markets, and uncertain economic conditions. The result might be confusion about what you actually want professionally versus what you think you should want.

Many millennials have complicated relationships with career authenticity because you entered the workforce during a time when both "follow your passion" culture and "hustle harder" mentality dominated career advice. These seemingly opposite approaches often create internal conflict between authentic interests and survival concerns.

Moving Past Toxic Productivity

Your generation has been particularly affected by productivity culture that treats busyness as virtue and rest as laziness. Social media amplified this by making everyone's work achievements visible and comparable. The result is often career choices driven more by external metrics than internal satisfaction.

Toxic Productivity Patterns:

Optimization Obsession: Treating every aspect of work life as something to hack, improve, or maximize rather than simply engaging authentically with your actual interests and capabilities.

Burnout as Badge: Viewing exhaustion, overwork, and stress as evidence of dedication rather than signs that something needs adjustment in your approach to career.

Passion Performance: Feeling pressure to be enthusiastic about your work all the time, even when you're going through natural periods of lower motivation or when your job simply pays the bills while serving other life priorities.

Success Theater: Focusing more energy on appearing successful (social media posts about achievements, networking events, professional image management) than on doing work that feels meaningful.

Productivity Guilt: Feeling guilty during downtime, vacation, or any period when you're not actively advancing your career, even when rest would improve your long-term effectiveness.

One person recognized their productivity toxicity: "I was working 60-hour weeks and constantly talking about how busy I was, like it proved I was important. But I realized I was using busyness to avoid facing the fact that I didn't actually like my work. Being constantly exhausted gave me an excuse not to pursue what I really wanted because I didn't have energy for anything else."

Aligning Work with Personal Values

Authentic career choices involve understanding what you actually value rather than what you think you should value based on family expectations, cultural messages, or economic pressures. This doesn't mean every job needs to be your dream career, but it does mean making conscious choices about how your work fits into your broader life priorities.

Common Value-Work Misalignments:

Autonomy vs. Structure: You might value independence but work in highly supervised environments, or prefer clear guidelines but work in ambiguous situations without enough direction.

Collaboration vs. Competition: Your natural working style might emphasize teamwork and mutual support, but your workplace culture rewards individual achievement and internal competition.

Creativity vs. Efficiency: You might be energized by innovation and creative problem-solving but work in roles that prioritize following established procedures and minimizing risk.

Impact vs. Income: You might be motivated by making a meaningful contribution but need higher income than mission-driven organizations typically provide, or vice versa.

Growth vs. Stability: Your development needs might require taking risks and trying new approaches, but your financial situation demands predictable income and benefits.

Exercise: Career Authenticity Assessment

This exercise helps you identify where your current career aligns with your authentic values and interests, and where there might be room for adjustment toward greater authenticity.

Step 1: Values Clarification

Write about what you actually value in work, separate from what you think you should value:

- What aspects of work feel most energizing and engaging to you?

- What work activities make you lose track of time in a positive way?

- What kind of work environment helps you feel most like yourself?

- What impact do you want your work to have, whether directly or through income that supports your other priorities?

- How important are factors like autonomy, collaboration, creativity, security, recognition, service, etc.?

Which work values feel most authentic to who you are rather than who you think you should be?

How do these values compare to what you prioritized when making current career decisions?

Step 2: Current Career Authenticity Audit

Honestly assess how your current work situation aligns with your authentic values:

- Which aspects of your job energize you versus drain you?

- When do you feel most like yourself at work versus when do you feel like you're performing a role?

- How much of your natural personality, interests, and strengths get expressed in your work?

- What work tasks or responsibilities do you consistently avoid or procrastinate on?

- How does your work support or conflict with your broader life priorities?

Where does your current career serve your authentic self versus where does it require suppressing important aspects of who you are?

What would need to change for your work to feel more aligned with your values?

Step 3: The Ideal Career Visualization

Spend 10-15 minutes visualizing your ideal career situation, ignoring practical constraints for now:

- What would you be doing day-to-day if money, education requirements, and others' expectations weren't factors?

- How would you prefer to use your natural talents and interests professionally?

- What kind of impact would you want your work to have?

- What would your ideal work environment and schedule look like?

- How would work fit into your overall lifestyle and priorities?

What elements of this ideal career vision feel most important to you?

Which aspects might be more achievable than you initially assume?

Step 4: Authentic Career Planning

Based on your assessment, identify 2-3 specific changes that could move your career toward greater authenticity:

- Modifications you could make within your current role

- Skills or experiences you could develop that align with your authentic interests

- Career transitions you could begin planning, even if they take time

- Ways to bring more of your authentic self into your current work

- Lifestyle or financial changes that could support more authentic career choices

What would be the first small step toward greater career authenticity?

What support or resources would help you make these changes?

Reflection Questions

How has hustle culture affected your relationship with work and rest?

What would change about your career choices if you fully trusted that you deserve work that aligns with your values?

How do you balance authentic career desires with practical financial needs?

What would you pursue professionally if you weren't worried about others' opinions or expectations?

Finding Meaningful Work Paths

Creating authentic career paths often involves integration rather than dramatic career changes. This might mean finding ways to express your values within existing roles, developing side projects that feed your authentic interests, or making gradual transitions toward more aligned work over time.

Strategies for Career Authenticity:

Incremental Alignment: Make small changes consistently rather than waiting for perfect opportunities. This might involve volunteering in areas that interest you, taking on different responsibilities in your current role, or developing skills that could lead to more authentic work.

Portfolio Approach: Consider combining different income sources that together create a career that serves your various interests and needs. This might include part-time work, freelancing, creative projects, and traditional employment in different combinations.

Values Integration: Find ways to express your authentic values within whatever work you're doing. Someone who values creativity might find ways to innovate within a traditional role, or someone who values service might volunteer while working a job primarily for financial reasons.

Lifestyle Design: Design your overall lifestyle to support the kind of career you want, which might involve geographic choices, financial decisions, or relationship considerations that create more career flexibility.

Long-term Planning: Make career decisions based on where you want to be in 5-10 years rather than just immediate circumstances, while accepting that plans will evolve as you grow and circumstances change.

Working with Career Anxiety

Career authenticity often triggers anxiety because it involves making choices based on internal rather than external validation. This can feel risky, especially when economic security feels precarious or when others don't understand your choices.

Common Career Authenticity Fears:

- Not earning enough money if you follow authentic interests
- Disappointing family or others who have expectations about your career
- Discovering that your authentic interests don't translate into viable career paths
- Being seen as impractical or unrealistic about work
- Giving up security for authenticity and regretting it

Managing Career Transition Anxiety:

- Make changes gradually rather than sudden dramatic shifts
- Develop multiple skills and income sources to reduce risk
- Connect with others who have made similar career transitions
- Save money to create financial buffer for career exploration
- Accept that some uncertainty is normal when pursuing authentic paths

Daily Integration

Today, identify one small way you could bring more of your authentic self into your current work situation. This might involve expressing an idea you usually keep to yourself, volunteering for a project that aligns with your interests, or simply being more genuinely yourself in work interactions.

Pay attention to which work activities energize you versus drain you, and consider what this tells you about alignment with your authentic interests and strengths. Notice when you feel like you're performing a professional role versus when you feel like you're expressing your natural capabilities.

Also consider your relationship with productivity and busyness. Are you working from genuine engagement or from anxiety about not doing enough? Practice taking breaks without guilt and focusing on quality of work rather than quantity of hours.

Tomorrow's Preparation

As you move through today, notice opportunities for creative expression, even in small ways. Pay attention to moments when you feel inspired to create, build, or express something artistic. These observations will help us explore creativity as a tool for shadow integration tomorrow.

Armed with this understanding, you're ready to explore how creative expression can become a powerful tool for integrating shadow aspects and expressing your authentic self more fully.

Day 20: Creative Expression as Shadow Integration

Daily Check-In

Before starting any tasks or checking your schedule, take a moment to imagine doing something purely creative today—something with no practical purpose except the joy of creating. What comes up for you? Excitement, resistance, guilt about "wasting time," or perhaps a longing you've been ignoring? Notice whatever arises without judging it.

You probably used to create things regularly without thinking about whether they were good, useful, or worth sharing. Maybe you drew pictures, wrote stories, built things, or made up songs just because it felt good. At some point, creativity might have become something you judged, compared to others, or felt you needed to be "good at" before it was worth doing.

Creative expression offers a unique pathway for shadow integration because it bypasses the rational mind and allows unconscious material to emerge naturally. When you create without specific goals or expectations, parts of yourself that have been hidden can find safe expression through color, movement, sound, or words.

Art Therapy for Shadow Work

You don't need to be an artist or have any particular creative talent to use artistic expression for psychological healing and growth. Art therapy principles can be applied by anyone willing to create without judgment and pay attention to what emerges through the creative process.

How Creativity Accesses Shadow Material:

Non-Verbal Expression: Many shadow aspects exist below the level of language and can be accessed more easily through visual, kinesthetic, or auditory creation than through verbal processing.

Unconscious Symbolism: Creative work often spontaneously produces symbols, colors, themes, or images that represent unconscious psychological material without requiring conscious interpretation.

Emotional Release: The creative process can provide safe outlet for emotions that feel too intense, confusing, or socially unacceptable to express directly.

Integration Through Play: Creative activities engage the playful, experimental aspects of personality that can help integrate serious psychological material without overwhelming yourself.

Bypassing Inner Critic: When focused on the process of creating rather than the quality of results, you can access authentic expression without the interference of critical judgment.

One person discovered this through art: "I started doing collages just to relax, cutting pictures from magazines without any plan. But I noticed themes emerging that I hadn't been conscious of—lots of images about travel and freedom when I was feeling trapped in my job, or dark, heavy images when I was dealing with family issues. It was like my unconscious was speaking through the pictures I chose."

Using Creativity for Healing

Creative expression can facilitate shadow integration by providing a safe container for exploring and expressing parts of yourself that might be too overwhelming or confusing to approach directly. This doesn't require formal art training or expensive materials—the healing comes through the process of creation, not the quality of what's produced.

Shadow-Focused Creative Approaches:

Automatic Writing: Writing continuously without planning or editing, allowing whatever wants to emerge to flow onto paper. This can access thoughts and feelings that your conscious mind might censor.

Intuitive Art Making: Creating visual art based on feelings, sensations, or impulses rather than predetermined plans. This might involve abstract painting, collage, sculpture, or any medium that appeals to you.

Movement Expression: Dancing, stretching, or moving in ways that feel authentic to your current emotional state rather than following prescribed forms or techniques.

Sound Work: Humming, singing, making sounds, or playing instruments in ways that express feelings directly rather than trying to create recognizable music.

Creative Writing: Writing stories, poems, or journal entries from the perspective of different parts of yourself, including shadow aspects that don't usually get to speak.

Mixed Media Exploration: Combining different creative mediums in experimental ways, allowing the process to guide you rather than having specific artistic goals.

Exercise: Creative Shadow Project

This exercise guides you through creating an artistic expression of your shadow work process, helping you integrate insights from the past weeks while accessing new levels of self-understanding.

Step 1: Creative Medium Selection

Choose a creative medium that appeals to you right now, even if you have no experience with it. Consider:

- Visual art (drawing, painting, collage, photography)

- Writing (poetry, fiction, journaling, automatic writing)

- Movement (dance, stretching, physical expression)

- Sound (singing, humming, instrument playing, vocal expression)

- Craft activities (knitting, building, gardening, cooking)

- Mixed media combinations

Which creative activity feels most appealing or accessible today?

What draws you to this particular form of expression?

Step 2: Shadow Theme Selection

Review your shadow work discoveries from the past weeks and choose one theme to explore creatively:

- A specific shadow pattern you want to understand better

- An aspect of yourself you've been suppressing

- An internal conflict between different parts of your personality

- An emotion you have difficulty expressing directly

- A change or integration you're working toward

Which shadow aspect feels most ready for creative exploration?

How might creative expression help you understand or work with this pattern?

Step 3: The Creative Process

Set aside 30-45 minutes for uninterrupted creative time. Begin by setting an intention to explore your chosen shadow theme through creativity, then let the process unfold naturally:

- Start creating without a specific plan or goal

- Pay attention to what wants to emerge rather than controlling the outcome

- Notice colors, shapes, movements, or sounds that feel meaningful

- Allow yourself to make "mistakes" or go in unexpected directions

- Focus on the experience of creating rather than evaluating what you're making

What surprises you about what emerges through the creative process?

How does this feel different from your usual goal-oriented activities?

Step 4: Creative Reflection

After completing your creative work, spend time reflecting on the process and what emerged:

- What themes, symbols, or patterns do you notice in what you created?

- How did it feel to express this shadow aspect creatively?

- What new insights or understanding emerged through the creative process?

- How might this creative exploration inform your ongoing shadow work?

- What would you want to explore further through creative expression?

What did you learn about your shadow theme through creative expression that you might not have accessed through thinking or talking alone?

Reflection Questions

How has your relationship with creativity changed since childhood?

What prevents you from creating regularly, and how might these obstacles connect to your shadow patterns?

How might creative expression support your overall psychological well-being and growth?

What would change about your self-relationship if you regularly made time for non-productive creative activities?

Making Space for Authentic Expression

Integrating creativity into your life as a shadow work tool requires protecting it from the productivity and achievement pressures that often kill creative joy. This means creating time and space for expression that doesn't need to be good, useful, or shareable.

Protecting Creative Space:

Process Over Product: Focus on the experience of creating rather than what you produce. The psychological benefits come through engagement with creative process, not through creating impressive results.

Privacy Protection: Keep some creative work private, allowing yourself to explore freely without concern about others' reactions or judgments.

Regular Practice: Engage with creativity regularly in small ways rather than waiting for large blocks of free time or perfect conditions.

Judgment Suspension: Practice creating without evaluating or comparing your work to others. The inner critic often destroys creative flow before shadow material can emerge.

Experimentation Encouragement: Try different creative mediums and approaches without committing to becoming "good" at any particular one.

Integration with Daily Life: Find ways to bring creative expression into routine activities—cooking creatively, decorating your space, or adding artistic elements to work projects.

Creative Community and Sharing

While protecting some creative work for private exploration, connecting with others around creative expression can provide support for both artistic development and shadow integration work.

Finding Creative Community:

- Local art classes, writing groups, or maker spaces
- Online communities focused on creative process rather than professional achievement
- Friends who are interested in creative exploration and personal growth
- Therapeutic or healing-focused creative groups
- Skill-sharing opportunities where people teach each other creative techniques

Conscious Sharing:

- Share creative work when it feels genuinely expressing rather than seeking validation
- Find people who appreciate creative exploration rather than only polished results
- Use creative sharing as opportunity for authentic connection rather than performance
- Respect your own boundaries about what feels appropriate to share versus keep private

Daily Integration

Today, engage in at least 15 minutes of creative expression that has no purpose other than the enjoyment of creating. This might be doodling while on phone calls, humming or singing along to music, writing freely in a journal, or any other form of creative play that appeals to you.

Pay attention to any resistance that comes up around "wasting time" on non-productive activities. Notice how this resistance might connect to broader shadow patterns about worth, productivity, or permission to enjoy yourself.

Also consider how you might integrate small creative activities into your regular routine without needing to add major time commitments or expenses to your life.

Tomorrow's Preparation

Tonight, gather all your notes and materials from this week's shadow work. Tomorrow you'll be integrating your discoveries about active shadow work, personal power, self-sabotage, conscious communication, career authenticity, and creative expression into a comprehensive approach to living with your whole self.

This foundation creates room for a complete integration of everything you've discovered about working consciously with your shadow patterns to create a more authentic and empowered way of living.

Day 21: Week 3 Integration: Embracing Your Whole Self

Daily Check-In

Take a moment to acknowledge the internal work you've accomplished this week. You've learned to dialogue with unconscious aspects of yourself, explored sources of authentic power, identified self-sabotage patterns, practiced conscious communication, examined career authenticity, and used creativity for psychological integration. This represents a sophisticated level of self-awareness that most people never develop.

As you prepare to integrate this week's discoveries, notice any part of you that wants to minimize the significance of this work or rush ahead to the next stage without fully absorbing what you've learned. Integration takes time and patience with yourself as you practice applying these insights in daily life.

This week moved you from passive awareness of shadow patterns into active engagement with them. You've begun developing relationships with parts of yourself that were previously unconscious, and started experimenting with expressing more of your authentic self in relationships, work, and creative activities.

Integration Versus Elimination Approach

One of the most important insights from shadow work is that the goal isn't to eliminate problematic patterns, but to develop conscious relationships with all aspects of your personality. This integration approach recognizes that every part of yourself developed for good reasons and likely contains valuable qualities along with limiting behaviors.

Integration Principles:

Acceptance Before Change: You can't successfully modify patterns you haven't fully accepted as part of yourself. Fighting against shadow aspects usually strengthens them, while accepting them often naturally leads to their positive expression.

Both/And Thinking: Instead of seeing personality traits as either good or bad, integration involves recognizing that most qualities can be both helpful and problematic depending on context and expression.

Conscious Choice: The goal is expanding your range of responses rather than eliminating certain behaviors. Sometimes assertiveness is appropriate; sometimes accommodation serves the situation better. Integration gives you conscious choice about how to respond.

Wholeness Over Perfection: A complete personality includes light and shadow aspects. Trying to be perfect usually means hiding parts of yourself rather than developing genuine maturity and self-acceptance.

Process Orientation: Integration happens gradually through small, consistent choices rather than dramatic personality changes. Expect this work to unfold over months and years as you practice applying insights in various situations.

Exercise: Wholeness Visualization

This exercise helps you create a visual and felt sense of what it means to embrace your complete self, including shadow aspects that you're learning to work with consciously.

Step 1: Complete Self-Assessment

Review your notes from this week and create a comprehensive picture of who you are when you include both conscious and shadow aspects:

Your Conscious Qualities: The personality traits, values, and behaviors you readily acknowledge and express

Your Shadow Qualities: The traits, impulses, and capabilities you've been suppressing or hiding

Your Integration Goals: How you want to work with shadow aspects more consciously

Your Authentic Power: Sources of strength and capability you're learning to express

Your Creative Expression: Ways that creativity helps you integrate and express your whole self

What does your complete personality look like when you include both conscious and shadow aspects?

How might your shadow qualities actually complement your conscious traits?

Step 2: The Wholeness Visualization Process

Find a quiet, comfortable space and spend 15-20 minutes in guided visualization:

Close your eyes and imagine yourself as completely integrated—not perfect, but whole. See yourself moving through a typical day expressing both your conscious qualities and your integrated shadow aspects. How do you handle challenges when you have access to your full range of capabilities? How do you relate to others when you're not hiding parts of yourself? How does it feel to be authentic and powerful simultaneously?

What did you notice about yourself when operating from wholeness rather than just your "acceptable" qualities?

How did integration feel different from trying to be perfect or hiding shadow aspects?

Step 3: Integration Challenges Assessment

Honestly assess what makes integration challenging for you:

- Which shadow aspects still feel scary or dangerous to express?

- What situations trigger your old patterns of hiding or performing?

- How do others respond when you're more authentic, and how does their response affect you?

- What internal resistance do you notice to embracing your whole self?

- What support or resources would help you maintain integration practices?

Which integration challenges feel most significant for your continued growth?

How might these challenges also represent opportunities for deeper self-acceptance?

Step 4: Integration Practice Planning

Based on your assessment, choose 2-3 specific practices for continuing integration work:

- Daily or weekly check-ins with different aspects of yourself

- Situations where you want to practice expressing more authentic power

- Relationships where you could experiment with more conscious communication

- Creative activities that support ongoing self-expression and discovery

- Professional contexts where you want to bring more of your authentic self

What integration practices feel most sustainable and meaningful for your lifestyle?

How will you maintain consistency with these practices when motivation fluctuates?

Reflection Questions

How has your understanding of personal growth and self-improvement changed through shadow work?

What would your life look like if you fully embraced your complexity rather than trying to be simple or consistent?

How might accepting your shadow aspects actually make you more loving and compassionate toward others?

What would you create or contribute if you had access to your full range of capabilities and authentic self-expression?

Celebrating Complexity and Wholeness

Integration involves learning to appreciate the richness and complexity of human personality rather than trying to achieve simplicity or consistency. This means accepting that you might be both ambitious and lazy, both generous and selfish, both confident and insecure, depending on circumstances and your internal state.

Benefits of Embracing Complexity:

Increased Authenticity: When you accept contradictory aspects of yourself, you can be more genuine in relationships rather than maintaining a consistent persona that requires constant energy to sustain.

Enhanced Creativity: Creative work often emerges from the tension between different aspects of personality. Integration provides access to broader ranges of inspiration and expression.

Improved Relationships: When you accept your own complexity, you become more tolerant and understanding of others' contradictions and human imperfections.

Greater Resilience: Access to your full range of qualities provides more resources for handling challenges and adapting to changing circumstances.

Reduced Internal Conflict: Fighting against parts of yourself creates psychological tension. Integration channels that energy toward conscious growth and authentic expression.

Setting Ongoing Integration Intentions

Moving forward, integration becomes a lifestyle practice rather than a temporary project. This involves regularly checking in with yourself, adjusting your relationship with shadow patterns as they evolve, and maintaining awareness of how unconscious dynamics affect your choices.

Sustainable Integration Practices:

Regular Self-Check-ins: Schedule weekly or monthly time for reflection on how shadow patterns are showing up in your current life and how you want to work with them.

Integration Accountability: Work with friends, mentors, or professionals who support your growth and can help you recognize when old patterns are recurring.

Ongoing Creative Expression: Maintain creative practices that help you stay connected to authentic self-expression and provide outlets for processing psychological material.

Conscious Relationship Practices: Continue developing skills for authentic communication and conscious relationship building that support mutual growth rather than hiding shadow aspects.

Career and Life Alignment: Regularly assess how your external life supports or conflicts with your authentic self, making adjustments when possible toward greater alignment.

Working with Integration Setbacks

Integration isn't linear, and you'll likely have periods when old shadow patterns feel more prominent or when you revert to familiar ways of hiding parts of yourself. These setbacks are normal and provide valuable information about what triggers unconscious patterns and what additional support you might need.

Common Integration Challenges:

- Reverting to old patterns during stress or major life changes

- Feeling uncomfortable when others respond differently to your increased authenticity

- Doubting the value of integration work when it feels difficult or slow

- Struggling to maintain new behaviors when motivation decreases

- Feeling overwhelmed by the complexity of ongoing self-awareness

Working with Setbacks:

- Treat regression as information about what triggers unconscious patterns rather than evidence of failure

- Practice self-compassion during difficult periods rather than self-criticism about "not being integrated enough"

- Reconnect with support systems and practices that help you maintain awareness and growth

- Adjust integration goals to be more realistic and sustainable for your current circumstances

- Remember that integration is a lifelong process rather than a destination to achieve

Daily Integration

Today, practice moving through your routine activities with awareness of both your conscious and shadow aspects, allowing yourself to be authentically complex rather than trying to be consistent or perfect. Notice when you feel tempted to hide parts of yourself and experiment with gentle, appropriate expression of authentic qualities.

Spend time appreciating the full spectrum of who you are, including qualities that you've judged as problematic. Consider how these traits might serve you when expressed consciously rather than when operating unconsciously.

Also consider what support systems, practices, or resources would help you maintain integration work as you continue beyond this structured program.

Tomorrow's Preparation

As you begin the final week of this program, you'll be focusing on practical skills for maintaining shadow awareness and integration in your daily life. Prepare by considering what aspects of this work feel most valuable to maintain long-term and what challenges you anticipate in sustaining these practices.

Having cleared this conceptual space, you're ready to develop practical skills for living with shadow awareness on an ongoing basis, creating sustainable approaches to authenticity and wholeness that can evolve with you over time.

Day 22: Daily Shadow Awareness Check-ins

Daily Check-In

Before jumping into your usual morning routine, take a moment to notice how you're feeling right now—not just your mood, but your energy level, what you're looking forward to, what you're avoiding, and what parts of yourself feel most present today. This kind of internal awareness is the foundation of sustainable shadow work.

You've probably noticed that some days you feel more like yourself than others. Maybe some mornings you wake up confident and ready to take on challenges, while other days you feel smaller or more reactive. These variations aren't random—they often reflect which aspects of your personality are active and which might be suppressed or struggling for attention.

Creating daily practices for shadow awareness doesn't mean analyzing yourself constantly or turning every experience into a therapy session. It means developing gentle habits of self-awareness that help you recognize patterns, make more conscious choices, and maintain connection with your authentic self amid the demands of daily life.

Creating Sustainable Practices

The key to long-term shadow work is developing practices that fit realistically into your actual lifestyle rather than the idealized version of yourself that has unlimited time and perfect consistency. Sustainable practices are brief, flexible, and focused on awareness rather than complicated analysis.

Most people try to create elaborate self-improvement routines that work for a few weeks before falling apart under the pressure of real life. Effective shadow work practices are different because they're based on curiosity rather than achievement, and they adapt to your changing circumstances rather than requiring perfect conditions.

Principles of Sustainable Shadow Practices:

Brevity Over Depth: Five minutes of consistent awareness practice is more valuable than hour-long sessions that happen sporadically. Brief practices build sustainable habits without creating pressure or overwhelm.

Flexibility Over Rigidity: Practices that can adapt to different schedules, energy levels, and circumstances are more likely to persist long-term than rigid routines that fall apart when life gets complicated.

Curiosity Over Judgment: Approaches based on gentle curiosity about your patterns create less resistance than practices focused on fixing or improving yourself. The goal is awareness, not perfection.

Integration Over Isolation: Shadow awareness works best when woven into existing activities rather than requiring separate time blocks. This makes it more practical and helps transfer insights into real-life situations.

Morning and Evening Routines

Bookending your day with brief shadow awareness practices helps you stay connected to your authentic self while navigating external demands and social expectations. These don't need to be lengthy or complicated—even two-minute check-ins can make a significant difference in self-awareness and conscious choice-making.

Morning Shadow Check-In (2-5 minutes):

- Notice your current energy level and emotional state without trying to change it

- Identify which aspects of your personality feel most present or active today

- Set a gentle intention for how you want to show up in the world
- Acknowledge any parts of yourself that might need attention or care during the day

Evening Shadow Reflection (3-7 minutes):

- Review moments when you felt most and least like yourself during the day
- Notice any patterns in what triggered shadow responses or authentic expression
- Appreciate yourself for moments of conscious choice or authentic action
- Set intentions for integration or self-care based on what you observed

One person described their sustainable practice: "I just started checking in with myself while I brush my teeth in the morning and evening. I ask myself how I'm feeling and what I need today, or what I noticed about myself during the day. It takes maybe two minutes but it keeps me connected to myself in a way that feels natural and doable."

Exercise: Daily Shadow Barometer

This exercise helps you create a simple, sustainable system for tracking your shadow patterns and levels of authentic expression throughout each day.

Step 1: Creating Your Personal Barometer

Develop a simple rating system for tracking different aspects of your daily experience. Choose 3-4 areas that feel most relevant to your shadow work:

Sample Categories:

- Authenticity level (how much you felt like yourself)

- Energy level (how energized versus drained you felt)

- Shadow pattern activity (how much old patterns influenced your choices)

- Conscious choice-making (how often you acted from awareness versus autopilot)

- Emotional expression (how freely you expressed authentic feelings)

- Boundary maintenance (how well you honored your limits and needs)

Create a simple 1-5 scale for each category, where 1 represents the challenging end and 5 represents the ideal.

Which aspects of daily experience would be most helpful for you to track?

How could you make this tracking system simple enough to maintain consistently?

Step 2: Morning Intention Setting

Each morning, spend 2-3 minutes setting gentle intentions based on your current state and what you learned from previous days:

- Check your current levels in each category

- Notice what might affect your day (schedule, stress, social interactions)

- Set realistic intentions for conscious choice-making

- Identify any shadow patterns to be particularly aware of

What would realistic daily intentions look like based on your actual life circumstances?

Step 3: Evening Reflection Process

Each evening, spend 3-5 minutes reviewing your day and updating your barometer:

- Rate your experience in each category

- Notice any patterns between different categories (when authenticity is low, is energy also low?)

- Identify specific moments of conscious choice or shadow pattern activation

- Appreciate yourself for any growth or awareness, however small

What patterns do you notice between your morning intentions and evening observations?

Step 4: Weekly Pattern Recognition

Once per week, review your daily ratings to identify broader patterns:

- Which days tend to be highest/lowest in different categories?

- What circumstances or activities support authentic expression versus trigger shadow patterns?

- How do different categories influence each other?

- What adjustments might support better overall well-being and authenticity?

What weekly patterns emerge that could inform how you structure your time and energy?

Reflection Questions

How could daily shadow awareness practices realistically fit into your current lifestyle?

What would change about your daily experience if you maintained consistent connection to your authentic self?

Which aspects of yourself do you most want to stay conscious of in daily life?

How might brief self-awareness practices prevent larger problems or unconscious patterns from developing?

Quick Integration Techniques

When you notice shadow patterns arising during daily life, having quick techniques for integration can help you respond more consciously rather than being controlled by unconscious dynamics. These techniques are designed to be used in real-time during busy, stressful, or triggering situations.

The Pause Practice: When you notice strong emotional reactions, automatic responses, or familiar patterns activating, pause for three conscious breaths before responding. This brief space often provides enough awareness to choose a different response.

The Internal Check-In: Ask yourself "What part of me is responding right now?" This helps identify whether you're operating from conscious choice, shadow patterns, or reactive emotions.

The Authentic Need Assessment: When feeling triggered or uncomfortable, ask "What do I actually need right now?" This helps distinguish between surface reactions and deeper needs that could be addressed more directly.

The Values Compass: Before making decisions or responding to situations, briefly consider "What response would align with my authentic values?" This helps access conscious choice rather than automatic patterns.

The Energy Audit: Throughout the day, notice what activities, interactions, or thoughts energize you versus drain you. This provides ongoing feedback about authenticity and alignment.

Working with Resistance

You'll likely encounter internal resistance to maintaining daily shadow awareness practices, especially during stressful periods when unconscious patterns feel more comfortable than conscious choice-making. This resistance is normal and provides valuable information about how your psyche protects familiar patterns.

Common Forms of Resistance:

- Forgetting to do practices consistently
- Feeling like practices are taking too much time
- Convincing yourself that awareness isn't making a difference
- Avoiding practices when you're experiencing difficult emotions
- Judging yourself for not being more consistent or insightful

Working with Resistance Compassionately:

- Accept that resistance is part of the growth process rather than evidence of failure
- Adjust practices to be more realistic when resistance is high
- Use resistance as information about what aspects of shadow work feel threatening or overwhelming
- Return to practices gently after breaks rather than criticizing yourself for inconsistency
- Remember that even imperfect awareness is more valuable than unconscious patterns

Daily Integration

Today, experiment with the morning and evening check-in practices, keeping them brief and focused on curiosity rather than analysis.

Notice how even small amounts of self-awareness affect your choices and responses throughout the day.

Pay attention to moments when you feel most and least connected to your authentic self, and consider what circumstances support conscious living versus unconscious pattern activation.

Also practice one or two of the quick integration techniques when you notice strong reactions or automatic responses arising during daily activities.

Tomorrow's Preparation

As you go through today, notice situations that trigger strong emotional responses, stress, or familiar reactive patterns. Pay attention to your first impulses in these moments and what happens if you pause before responding. These observations will help us explore real-time trigger management tomorrow.

"Building these awareness muscles consistently creates the foundation for all other shadow work."

Having built this awareness muscle, you're ready to learn how to work with triggers and reactive patterns as they arise in real-time, rather than only processing them after the fact.

Day 23: Real-Time Trigger Management

Daily Check-In

Think about the last time someone or something triggered a strong emotional reaction in you—maybe anger, anxiety, hurt, or frustration that felt bigger than the situation seemed to warrant. In that moment, did you respond from the intensity of the trigger, or were you able to pause and choose your response consciously? Most people find that triggers happen faster than their ability to respond thoughtfully.

You've probably noticed that certain situations, people, or even thoughts can shift your emotional state dramatically within seconds. Maybe hearing criticism activates immediate defensiveness, or seeing certain social media content triggers comparison and inadequacy. These reactions often feel automatic and overwhelming, leaving you feeling controlled by external circumstances rather than responsive from your authentic self.

Learning to work with triggers in real-time is one of the most practical applications of shadow work. Instead of being controlled by unconscious reactions, you can develop skills for recognizing triggers as they arise and choosing how to respond based on your current values and goals rather than old patterns.

Using Triggers as Teachers

Traditional approaches to triggers often focus on avoiding them or controlling emotional reactions. Shadow work takes a different approach: triggers are valuable information about unconscious patterns, unhealed aspects of yourself, and areas where growth is possible. Instead of seeing triggers as problems, you can learn to see

186

them as teachers pointing toward shadow material that's ready for conscious attention.

What Triggers Reveal:

Unintegrated Shadow Aspects: Strong reactions often point to qualities in others that you've suppressed in yourself. If someone's confidence triggers insecurity, you might have suppressed your own natural confidence. If their neediness annoys you, you might be avoiding your own need for support.

Unmet Needs: Triggers often activate when core needs aren't being met or acknowledged. Anger might arise when your need for respect is ignored. Anxiety might emerge when your need for security feels threatened.

Old Wounds: Current situations sometimes trigger emotional reactions that are actually about past experiences. Understanding this can help you respond to present circumstances rather than react to historical pain.

Values Conflicts: Strong reactions can indicate situations where your values are being violated or compromised, either by others or by your own behavior.

Growth Edges: The situations that trigger you most intensely often represent areas where conscious development is most needed and most possible.

One person realized this about their triggers: "I always got really angry when people were late, way angrier than seemed reasonable. I thought it was just about disrespect, but I realized it triggered my childhood anxiety about unpredictability. Once I understood that, I could work with the underlying anxiety instead of just getting mad at people."

Millennial Stress Management Strategies

Your generation faces unique stressors that require updated approaches to trigger management. Traditional stress management techniques were designed for different social and economic conditions, and many don't address the specific challenges millennials navigate daily.

Millennial-Specific Stress Triggers:

Information Overload: Constant access to news, social media, and digital communication creates ongoing low-level stress that can make you more reactive to interpersonal triggers.

Economic Uncertainty: Job insecurity and financial pressure can make relatively small work conflicts or expenses feel much more threatening than they might during more stable times.

Social Comparison: Daily exposure to others' highlight reels can create chronic inadequacy feelings that make criticism or failure feel more devastating.

Future Anxiety: Uncertainty about climate, politics, and social stability can make present-moment triggers feel more intense because they're layered on top of ongoing worry about the future.

Relationship Complexity: Modern dating and friendship dynamics create unique interpersonal triggers around commitment, communication, and authenticity that previous generations didn't navigate.

Exercise: In-the-Moment Integration

This exercise teaches you specific techniques for working with triggers as they arise, helping you respond from awareness rather than react from unconscious patterns.

Step 1: Trigger Identification and Mapping

Identify your 3-5 most common trigger situations and understand their patterns:

Common Trigger Categories:

- Criticism or judgment from others

- Feeling ignored, dismissed, or devalued
- Situations involving conflict or confrontation
- Financial stress or money-related decisions
- Social comparison or feeling excluded
- Work pressure or performance evaluation
- Relationship uncertainty or rejection

For each trigger, write about:

- What typically happens in your body when this trigger arises
- What thoughts automatically go through your mind
- How you usually respond behaviorally
- What you think this trigger might be trying to tell you about unmet needs or shadow aspects

Which triggers feel most intense or difficult to manage consciously?

What patterns do you notice across different types of triggers?

Step 2: The STOP Technique Development

Create a personal protocol for pausing when triggers arise. The acronym STOP can help you remember the steps:

S - Stop: Notice the trigger activation and pause before responding
T - Take a breath: Use breath to create space between trigger and response
O - Observe: Notice what's happening internally without judging it
P - Proceed: Choose your response based on current values rather than automatic patterns

Practice this technique mentally with recent trigger situations, imagining how you could have used it.

How could you adapt this technique to work in your most common trigger situations?

Step 3: Real-Time Integration Practices

Develop specific practices for working with triggers as they happen:

Body Awareness: Learn to recognize the physical sensations that accompany your triggers—tension, heat, racing heart, shallow breathing. These physical cues often arise before emotional awareness.

Trigger Dialogue: Briefly ask the triggered part of yourself "What are you trying to protect me from?" or "What do you need me to know?" This accesses valuable information quickly.

Values Check-In: Ask yourself "How do I want to show up in this situation based on my authentic values?" This helps access conscious choice rather than reactive patterns.

Perspective Shift: Remind yourself "This person/situation is showing me something about my growth edge" rather than "This person/situation is doing something to me."

Which of these practices feels most accessible for you to use during actual trigger situations?

Step 4: Post-Trigger Integration

Develop a brief practice for learning from trigger experiences after they occur:

- What triggered you and how did you respond?

- What did you learn about your patterns or needs?

- How might you respond differently in similar future situations?

- What support or resources might help you work with this trigger more consciously?

How could you make post-trigger reflection a regular practice without it becoming self-criticism?

Reflection Questions

How do your trigger patterns connect to the shadow work you've been doing over the past three weeks?

What would change about your daily experience if you could respond to triggers from conscious choice rather than automatic reactions?

Which trigger management techniques feel most realistic and helpful for your actual lifestyle and stress levels?

How might working with triggers consciously improve your relationships and professional effectiveness?

Conscious Response Protocols

Developing conscious response protocols means having prepared strategies for common trigger situations rather than hoping you'll remember to respond differently in the heat of the moment. These protocols provide structure for accessing your values and authentic self when emotions are high.

Protocol for Criticism or Judgment:

1. Pause and breathe before defending or explaining

2. Ask yourself what valid information might be contained in the feedback

3. Respond to the content rather than the delivery or your emotional reaction

4. Thank the person for their input, even if you don't agree with it

5. Take time later to process whether any changes would serve you

Protocol for Comparison Triggers:

1. Notice the comparison arising without judging yourself for having it

2. Remind yourself that you're seeing limited information about others' complete experience

3. Redirect attention to your own progress and growth rather than relative position

4. Practice appreciation for something positive in your current situation

5. Limit exposure to comparison-triggering content when possible

Protocol for Conflict or Confrontation:

1. Notice your impulse to either fight back or withdraw completely

2. Ask yourself what you genuinely need from this situation

3. Express your perspective using "I" statements rather than accusations

4. Stay curious about the other person's experience rather than assuming their motivations

5. Focus on finding solutions rather than proving who's right

Working with Chronic Triggers

Some triggers arise so frequently or intensely that they significantly impact daily life and relationships. These chronic triggers often point to deeper shadow work that might benefit from additional support or more intensive attention.

Signs of Chronic Triggers:

- Same triggers arise repeatedly across different situations and relationships

- Trigger reactions are significantly disproportionate to present circumstances

- Triggers prevent you from engaging in activities or relationships that are important to you

- You find yourself organizing your life around avoiding certain triggers

- Trigger reactions include anxiety, rage, or despair that lasts for hours or days

Addressing Chronic Triggers:

- Consider working with a therapist who understands trauma and shadow work

- Explore whether chronic triggers connect to unresolved experiences from earlier in life

- Develop additional support systems for managing intense emotional reactions

- Practice extra self-compassion when working with deeply rooted patterns

- Accept that some triggers may take longer to integrate than others

Daily Integration

Today, practice the STOP technique when you notice any trigger arising, even small ones. Use minor irritations or stresses as opportunities to build skill with conscious response rather than waiting for major triggers to practice.

Pay attention to your body's signals throughout the day, noticing physical tension, energy changes, or emotional shifts that might indicate triggers before they become overwhelming reactions.

Also experiment with curiosity about what your triggers might be teaching you, treating them as information about your growth edges rather than problems to eliminate.

Tomorrow's Preparation

As you move through today, notice situations where you feel pressure to say yes when you'd prefer to say no, or where you accommodate others at the expense of your own needs or boundaries. Pay attention to how you feel before, during, and after these interactions. These observations will help us explore authentic boundary setting tomorrow.

With these tools in your toolkit, you're ready to learn how conscious trigger management supports another crucial aspect of authentic living: setting and maintaining healthy boundaries from a place of wholeness rather than defensive reactivity.

Day 24: Authentic Boundary Setting

Daily Check-In

Before interacting with anyone today, take a moment to check in with your current energy level and emotional capacity. What do you genuinely have available to give to others today? What do you need to protect or conserve for yourself? Notice whether assessing your own limits feels natural and caring, or whether it brings up guilt or anxiety about being selfish.

You've probably found yourself saying yes to requests when you wanted to say no, or accommodating others' needs while ignoring your own clear signals that you're overwhelmed or uncomfortable. Maybe you've noticed that some people seem to respect your time and energy automatically, while others consistently push against your limits until you either give in or become resentful.

Healthy boundaries aren't walls that keep people out—they're conscious choices about how to use your energy, time, and emotional resources in ways that support both your well-being and your ability to show up authentically in relationships. When boundaries come from wholeness rather than defensiveness, they actually improve relationships by creating clarity and preventing resentment.

Boundary Setting from Wholeness

Traditional boundary-setting advice often focuses on protecting yourself from other people, as if relationships were fundamentally threatening and boundaries were primarily defensive. Shadow work approaches boundaries differently: they're expressions of self-respect and clarity about your authentic needs that actually enable deeper connection with others.

Boundaries from Wholeness vs. Defensive Boundaries:

Wholeness-Based Boundaries come from knowing yourself well enough to be clear about your limits, needs, and values. They feel calm and grounded rather than reactive. You can set them with compassion for both yourself and others because you're not fighting against parts of yourself.

Defensive Boundaries often arise from fear, resentment, or unintegrated shadow aspects. They might be too rigid (keeping everyone at distance) or too permeable (allowing others to violate your limits). They often feel emotionally charged because they're protecting against perceived threats rather than expressing authentic preferences.

Characteristics of Authentic Boundaries:

- Clear without being harsh or punitive

- Consistent across different relationships and situations

- Based on your actual limits and needs rather than what you think you should need

- Maintained with self-compassion rather than self-criticism when you occasionally struggle with them

- Flexible enough to adapt to different circumstances while maintaining core principles

One person described learning authentic boundaries: "I used to think boundaries meant being mean to people or cutting them off completely. But I learned that real boundaries are actually kind—they help people understand how to have a good relationship with me instead of leaving them to guess what I need."

Saying No with Compassion

Many millennials struggle with saying no because you were raised to be considerate and helpful, often during times when family systems needed extra support due to economic stress or other challenges. Learning to decline requests without guilt or elaborate explanations is a crucial skill for maintaining authentic boundaries.

The Challenge of Millennial No-Saying:

- Economic uncertainty can make saying no to professional opportunities feel risky

- Social media makes it visible when you say no to some invitations but yes to others

- Family financial interdependence can make boundaries feel like ingratitude

- Dating culture encourages being low-maintenance and agreeable

- Friend groups often expect high availability and immediate responses

Compassionate No-Saying Strategies:

Direct and Brief: "I won't be able to do that" is a complete sentence. You don't need to justify your boundaries with elaborate explanations that invite negotiation.

Acknowledge the Request: "Thanks for thinking of me, but I can't take this on right now" shows appreciation while maintaining your boundary.

Offer Alternatives When Appropriate: If you genuinely want to help but can't meet the specific request, you might suggest other ways to support or different timing.

Express Your Limits Neutrally: "I don't have bandwidth for that" or "That doesn't work for my schedule" focuses on your limitations rather than judging the request.

Stay Kind but Firm: Compassion doesn't require sacrificing your boundaries. You can be caring toward others while still honoring your limits.

Exercise: Boundary Practice Scenarios

This exercise helps you develop specific language and strategies for setting boundaries in common situations while maintaining relationships and self-respect.

Step 1: Personal Boundary Assessment

Identify your current boundary challenges by assessing different areas of life:

Work Boundaries:

- Do you regularly work beyond your stated hours?

- Can you say no to additional projects when you're already overwhelmed?

- Do you check work email during personal time?

- Can you take breaks and vacation without guilt?

Social Boundaries:

- Do you attend events you don't want to attend to avoid disappointing others?

- Can you leave social situations when you're tired or uncomfortable?

- Do you feel obligated to respond immediately to texts and calls?

- Can you express different opinions without excessive worry about others' reactions?

Family Boundaries:

- Can you limit family time when you need space for other priorities?

- Do you feel comfortable having different values or lifestyle choices than family members?

- Can you avoid getting pulled into family conflicts or drama?

- Do you feel free to make major life decisions without family approval?

Financial Boundaries:

- Can you say no to requests for money when lending would strain your budget?

- Do you feel comfortable spending money on yourself without justifying it to others?

- Can you avoid financial decisions that primarily benefit others at your expense?

Which areas feel most challenging for boundary setting?

What patterns do you notice in where boundaries feel easier versus more difficult?

Step 2: Boundary Language Development

For each challenging area, develop specific language for setting boundaries that feels authentic to your communication style:

Sample Boundary Statements:

- "I care about you and I won't be able to help with this"

- "That doesn't work for me, but I hope you find a good solution"

- "I'm not available for that kind of conversation"

- "I need to think about it before I can give you an answer"

- "I appreciate the invitation, but I won't be able to make it"

- "I understand this is important to you, and I have different priorities right now"

Practice saying these phrases out loud until they feel natural and authentic to your voice.

Which boundary statements feel most comfortable for you to use?

How might you adapt this language for different relationships and situations?

Step 3: Boundary Challenge Scenarios

Practice setting boundaries in specific situations that typically challenge you:

Scenario Practice: Write out how you would handle each situation using authentic boundary language:

- A colleague asks you to cover their work when you're already behind on your own projects

- A friend consistently cancels plans at the last minute but expects you to always be available when they want to hang out

- Family members criticize your life choices and want to discuss how you should change them

- Someone asks to borrow money when you can't afford to lend it

- You're invited to an event that conflicts with something you'd rather do or with time you need for rest

What feels most challenging about each scenario?

How might you maintain the relationship while still honoring your boundaries?

Step 4: Boundary Maintenance Planning

Develop strategies for maintaining boundaries when they're tested or when you feel pressure to abandon them:

- How will you respond when someone pushes back against your boundaries?

- What support systems help you stay consistent with boundary-setting?

- How will you handle guilt or anxiety that arises when setting boundaries?

- What signs indicate that you need to reassess or strengthen certain boundaries?

What makes it hardest for you to maintain boundaries once you've set them?

What resources or practices would support consistent boundary maintenance?

Reflection Questions

How do your boundary challenges connect to the shadow patterns you've been exploring?

What would change about your relationships if you consistently honored your authentic limits and needs?

How might healthy boundaries actually improve your ability to be generous and caring toward others?

What would you have more energy for if you weren't constantly managing other people's reactions or needs?

Protecting Energy Authentically

Authentic boundary setting involves understanding your actual energy patterns and capacity rather than trying to meet abstract standards about what you should be able to handle. This requires ongoing awareness of what energizes you versus what drains you, and making choices that support your long-term well-being rather than just managing immediate situations.

Energy Protection Strategies:

Energy Auditing: Regularly assess which activities, people, and commitments energize you versus drain you. This information helps you make conscious choices about how to spend your time and attention.

Proactive Boundary Setting: Set boundaries before you're overwhelmed rather than waiting until you're already depleted and resentful. This is easier on both you and the people around you.

Recovery Time Planning: Build time for rest and restoration into your schedule rather than treating it as something that happens only when everything else is finished.

Social Energy Management: Balance social time with alone time based on your actual needs rather than social expectations about how much interaction is normal or healthy.

Digital Boundaries: Manage your exposure to news, social media, and digital communication in ways that protect your mental and emotional well-being.

Working with Boundary Guilt

Many people experience guilt when setting boundaries, especially if they're used to prioritizing others' comfort over their own well-being. This guilt often comes from inherited programming about what makes someone good, caring, or valuable in relationships.

Common Sources of Boundary Guilt:

- Believing that caring for yourself is selfish

- Fear that others will be hurt or angry if you prioritize your needs

- Worry that people will think you're being difficult or demanding

- Feeling responsible for managing others' emotions and reactions

- Confusion between being kind and being available for everything others want

Working with Boundary Guilt Compassionately:

- Remember that guilt doesn't mean you're doing something wrong—it often means you're changing patterns that no longer serve you

- Practice distinguishing between appropriate responsibility (your choices and actions) and inappropriate responsibility (others' feelings and reactions)

- Notice how boundary-setting actually improves relationships by creating clarity and preventing resentment

- Start with smaller boundaries to build confidence before addressing larger ones

- Connect with others who support your growth rather than only people who benefit from your lack of boundaries

Daily Integration

Today, practice setting one small boundary that you've been avoiding. This might be saying no to a request, limiting time spent on an activity that drains you, or expressing a preference that you usually keep to yourself.

Pay attention to how boundary-setting feels in your body—notice whether it creates tension, relief, anxiety, or other sensations. Often the physical experience can guide you toward authentic boundaries.

Also notice how others respond when you set clear, kind boundaries. Most people respect boundaries when they're expressed calmly and consistently, even if they're initially disappointed.

Tomorrow's Preparation

As you move through your day, notice moments when you have opportunities to influence others—through your work, relationships, or community involvement. Pay attention to when you step into leadership roles versus when you hold back from expressing your ideas or taking initiative. These observations will help us explore authentic leadership from wholeness tomorrow.

As this understanding settles, you're ready to explore how the self-awareness and boundary-setting skills you've developed can support authentic leadership that influences others while staying true to your whole self.

Day 25: Millennial Leadership from Wholeness

Daily Check-In

Think about a time when you felt genuinely inspired by someone's leadership—not because they had authority or power over you, but because they influenced you to be more yourself or to engage with something meaningful. What qualities did they demonstrate? How did their leadership feel different from people who tried to control or impress others? Notice whether you recognize any of those leadership qualities within yourself.

You might not think of yourself as a leader, especially if you picture leadership as requiring formal authority, charismatic personality, or confidence you don't always feel. But leadership happens anytime you influence others toward positive change, whether that's through your work, relationships, community involvement, or simply how you show up in the world.

Millennial leadership often looks different from previous generations' models because you're leading during a time of rapid change, systemic challenges, and evolving values around collaboration, authenticity, and social responsibility. This creates opportunities for more conscious, inclusive forms of leadership that integrate rather than suppress different aspects of personality and values.

Conscious Leadership Principles

Traditional leadership models often emphasized projection of confidence, control of outcomes, and maintenance of authority through hierarchy and expertise. Conscious leadership integrates these practical elements with self-awareness, emotional intelligence, and recognition that sustainable influence comes through authentic connection rather than domination.

Core Principles of Conscious Leadership:

Self-Awareness as Foundation: Conscious leaders understand their own patterns, triggers, strengths, and limitations. This self-knowledge helps them make better decisions, communicate more effectively, and avoid projecting their unconscious issues onto others.

Authenticity Over Performance: Instead of performing an idealized leadership persona, conscious leaders show up as themselves while adapting their communication and approach to serve different situations and people.

Collaboration Over Control: Conscious leadership recognizes that complex challenges require diverse perspectives and skills. The leader's role becomes facilitating collective wisdom rather than having all the answers.

Growth Orientation: Conscious leaders view challenges, failures, and conflicts as opportunities for learning and development rather than threats to their authority or competence.

Values Alignment: Conscious leaders make decisions based on clearly articulated values rather than just immediate outcomes or external expectations.

Service Motivation: The primary motivation is contributing to something meaningful rather than personal advancement or recognition, though personal growth and achievement can be natural byproducts.

One person described discovering their leadership style: "I always thought I wasn't leadership material because I'm not naturally commanding or super confident. But I realized I influence people through listening carefully, asking good questions, and helping them connect with their own insights. That's actually a powerful form of leadership, even though it doesn't look like what I expected."

Authentic Influence Strategies

Authentic influence happens when people are inspired to change or grow because they trust your motives and respect your integrity, rather than because they fear consequences or want to gain your approval. This type of influence is sustainable because it's based on genuine connection rather than manipulation or performance.

Millennial-Specific Leadership Strengths:

Systems Thinking: Your generation grew up understanding interconnectedness through technology and global awareness. This creates natural ability to see how different elements affect each other and to address root causes rather than just symptoms.

Collaborative Instincts: Growing up with social media and group projects created comfort with shared decision-making and collective problem-solving that older generations sometimes struggle with.

Values Integration: Millennials often refuse to separate personal values from professional behavior, creating more authentic and consistent leadership approaches.

Change Adaptability: Having lived through multiple economic and social disruptions, your generation developed flexibility and resilience that serves leadership in uncertain times.

Inclusive Awareness: Growing up in more diverse environments created awareness of different perspectives and experiences that supports inclusive leadership approaches.

Authenticity Expectation: Having been raised to "be yourself," millennials often have less tolerance for fake or performative leadership and more skill at authentic communication.

Exercise: Leadership Shadow Integration

This exercise helps you identify your natural leadership qualities, understand how shadow patterns might interfere with authentic influence, and develop approaches to leadership that integrate your whole self.

Step 1: Leadership Style Assessment

Explore your natural leadership tendencies and preferences:

Leadership Reflection Questions:

- When do you naturally step into influencing or guiding roles?
- What leadership qualities do others consistently recognize in you?
- How do you prefer to motivate and inspire others?
- What kind of environments bring out your best leadership capabilities?
- When do you hold back from leadership opportunities, and why?
- What leadership approaches feel most and least authentic to you?

What patterns do you notice in when and how you naturally lead others?

Which leadership qualities feel most authentic to your personality and values?

Step 2: Leadership Shadow Exploration

Identify how shadow patterns might affect your leadership effectiveness:

Common Leadership Shadows:

- **Impostor Syndrome**: Believing you're not qualified to lead despite evidence of your capabilities
- **People-Pleasing**: Avoiding difficult decisions or conversations to maintain approval

208

- **Perfectionism**: Setting unrealistic standards that create stress for yourself and others

- **Control Issues**: Micromanaging because you don't trust others to meet your standards

- **Conflict Avoidance**: Preventing necessary difficult conversations that would improve team effectiveness

- **Recognition Hunger**: Leading primarily for external validation rather than service to meaningful goals

Which shadow patterns most interfere with your natural leadership capabilities?

How might these patterns both protect and limit your influence with others?

Step 3: Authentic Leadership Vision

Create a clear picture of how you want to show up as a leader when integrating your whole self:

- What impact do you want to have on people you lead or influence?

- What values do you want to demonstrate consistently through your leadership?

- How do you want to handle conflict, failure, and difficult decisions?

- What kind of culture or environment do you want to create through your influence?

- How will you balance confidence with humility, strength with vulnerability?

What would leadership look like if you expressed your authentic self while serving others effectively?

Step 4: Leadership Development Planning

Based on your assessment, identify specific ways to develop more conscious leadership:

- Situations where you could practice stepping into leadership more authentically

- Skills or knowledge that would support your natural leadership style

- Shadow work that would improve your leadership effectiveness

- Mentors or role models who demonstrate leadership approaches you admire

- Ways to gain leadership experience that align with your values and interests

What would be the most meaningful next step in developing your authentic leadership capabilities?

Reflection Questions

How do your ideas about leadership differ from traditional models you observed growing up?

What would change about your professional and personal relationships if you fully owned your leadership capabilities?

How might your shadow work enhance your ability to influence others positively?

What kind of change do you most want to create through your leadership influence?

Creating Positive Change

Millennial leadership often focuses on creating positive change in systems, organizations, or communities rather than just managing existing structures. This requires skills for identifying problems, building coalitions, and implementing solutions that address root causes rather than just surface symptoms.

Strategies for Change-Oriented Leadership:

Start with Personal Integration: The most effective change agents do their own shadow work and personal development. You can't lead others toward growth you haven't done yourself.

Build Authentic Relationships: Sustainable change happens through genuine connection and trust. Invest time in understanding others' perspectives and needs rather than just promoting your ideas.

Address Systems, Not Just Symptoms: Look for underlying patterns that create problems rather than just addressing individual incidents. Millennial systems thinking is valuable for this approach.

Communicate Vision Clearly: Help others understand not just what needs to change, but why it matters and how it connects to values they care about.

Model the Change: Demonstrate the behaviors, attitudes, and approaches you want to see others adopt rather than just talking about what should be different.

Build Collective Capacity: Develop others' leadership capabilities rather than trying to be the only person driving change. Sustainable transformation requires distributed leadership.

Working with Leadership Anxiety

Many millennials experience anxiety about taking leadership roles because of economic uncertainty, impostor syndrome, or concerns about being too young or inexperienced. These anxieties often prevent valuable leadership from emerging when it's needed most.

Common Leadership Anxieties:

- Fear of making mistakes that affect others

- Worry about not having enough experience or expertise

- Anxiety about being criticized or judged by people you're trying to lead

- Concern about the responsibility and pressure that comes with influence

- Fear of conflict or difficult conversations that leadership often requires

Working with Leadership Anxiety Constructively:

- Accept that some anxiety is normal when taking on meaningful responsibility

- Start with smaller leadership opportunities to build confidence gradually

- Focus on service to others rather than personal performance or image

- Connect with mentors who can provide guidance and support

- Remember that leadership is a skill that develops through practice, not something you need to be perfect at immediately

Daily Integration

Today, look for one opportunity to practice authentic leadership, even in a small way. This might mean speaking up in a meeting, offering to help organize something, expressing a vision for improvement, or simply modeling behavior you'd like to see others adopt.

Pay attention to how it feels to step into influence consciously rather than waiting for others to take initiative. Notice what supports your authentic leadership and what triggers insecurity or performance anxiety.

Also consider how your shadow work over the past weeks might enhance your leadership effectiveness by helping you stay conscious and authentic under pressure.

Tomorrow's Preparation

As you engage with social media today, notice how you present yourself online and how you feel while scrolling through various platforms. Pay attention to moments when social media supports authentic connection versus when it triggers comparison or performance pressure. These observations will help us explore conscious social media engagement tomorrow.

From this place of knowing, you're ready to apply the authenticity and conscious choice-making you've been developing to your digital life, creating online presence that reflects your whole self rather than a curated performance.

Day 26: Conscious Social Media Engagement

Daily Check-In

Before opening any social media apps today, pause and notice your internal state. What are you hoping to get from social media right now? Connection? Entertainment? Distraction? Information? Validation? There's no right answer, but awareness of your intention can help you use these platforms more consciously rather than mindlessly scrolling out of habit.

You probably have a complex relationship with social media— appreciating the connection and information it provides while also recognizing how it can trigger comparison, anxiety, or time-wasting patterns. Maybe you've noticed that some social media sessions leave you feeling energized and connected, while others leave you drained or inadequate.

Conscious social media engagement means using these platforms in ways that support your authentic self-expression and genuine connection rather than feeding shadow patterns or unconscious habits. This doesn't require eliminating social media, but it does mean bringing intentionality to how and why you engage with digital platforms.

Digital Life with Shadow Awareness

Social media platforms are designed to capture attention and encourage engagement, often by triggering psychological patterns like comparison, fear of missing out, validation-seeking, and compulsive checking. Understanding how these platforms interact with your shadow patterns helps you use them more consciously.

How Social Media Activates Shadow Patterns:

Comparison Triggers: Constant exposure to others' highlight reels can activate inadequacy feelings and competitive patterns, especially if you've suppressed confidence or self-appreciation.

Validation Seeking: The metrics of likes, comments, and shares can trigger parts of yourself that learned to measure worth through external approval rather than internal satisfaction.

Performance Pressure: The knowledge that posts are permanent and visible creates pressure to present an optimized version of yourself rather than authentic expression.

FOMO Activation: Seeing others' activities and opportunities can trigger anxiety about your own choices and fear that you're missing out on better experiences.

Perfectionism Reinforcement: The ability to edit, filter, and curate content perfectly can strengthen perfectionist patterns rather than supporting acceptance of natural human imperfection.

One person described their social media shadow awareness: "I realized I was posting pictures not because I wanted to share experiences, but because I needed proof that my life was interesting enough. I was using social media to manage my insecurity instead of actually enjoying my experiences."

Exercise: Social Media Audit

This exercise helps you assess your current social media patterns and identify changes that would support more authentic digital engagement.

Step 1: Usage Pattern Analysis

For the next 2-3 days, pay attention to your actual social media behavior:

Tracking Questions:

- How often do you check each platform throughout the day?

- What triggers you to open social media apps (boredom, anxiety, habit, specific intentions)?

- How do you typically feel before, during, and after social media sessions?

- What types of content do you engage with most (likes, comments, shares)?

- How much time do you spend scrolling versus actively connecting with others?

What patterns do you notice in when and why you use social media?

How does social media use affect your mood and energy throughout the day?

Step 2: Content Impact Assessment

Evaluate how different types of social media content affect you:

Content Categories to Assess:

- Friends' personal updates and life events

- News and political content

- Inspirational or motivational posts

- Entertainment and humor content

- Professional or career-related posts

- Advertising and promotional content

- Celebrity or influencer content

For each category, notice:

- Does this content generally energize or drain you?

- Does it trigger comparison, anxiety, or other uncomfortable emotions?

- Does it inspire positive action or just passive consumption?

- Does it support authentic connection or create distance from real relationships?

Which types of content most support your well-being and authentic self-expression?

What content consistently triggers shadow patterns or negative emotional states?

Step 3: Posting and Sharing Analysis

Examine your own social media posting patterns:

- What do you typically share, and what do you avoid sharing?

- How do you decide what's appropriate to post?

- How do you feel while creating posts versus after they're published?

- How much do engagement metrics (likes, comments) affect your mood?

- When do you post from authentic expression versus seeking validation?

What motivates your posting behavior—genuine sharing or performance for others?

How might you post more authentically while still respecting appropriate boundaries?

Reflection Questions

How has social media shaped your sense of what constitutes a normal or successful life?

What would change about your social media use if you weren't concerned about others' judgments or approval?

How might conscious social media engagement support your shadow integration work?

What role do you want digital platforms to play in your authentic relationships and self-expression?

Building Genuine Connections

Social media can support authentic relationships when used consciously, but this requires approaching it as a tool for real connection rather than performance or passive entertainment consumption.

Strategies for Authentic Digital Connection:

Quality Over Quantity: Engage meaningfully with fewer people rather than broadcasting to large audiences. Comment thoughtfully on friends' posts, send private messages, and use social media to deepen existing relationships.

Share Authentically: Post content that reflects your genuine interests, experiences, and values rather than what you think will get the most engagement. This attracts people who appreciate your actual personality.

Ask Questions: Use social media to learn about others' experiences rather than just sharing your own. Curiosity about others creates more genuine connection than self-promotion.

Support Others Consciously: Use your engagement to lift others up rather than just seeking attention for yourself. Meaningful comments and encouragement create positive social media culture.

Direct Communication: When social media interactions reveal someone you'd like to know better, move conversations to direct messages, phone calls, or in-person meetings when possible.

Protecting Mental Health Online

Conscious social media use includes protecting your mental and emotional well-being by setting boundaries around content that consistently triggers negative reactions or shadow patterns.

Digital Wellness Strategies:

Curate Consciously: Unfollow or mute accounts that consistently trigger comparison, anxiety, or other negative emotions. Your social media feed should generally support your well-being rather than undermine it.

Time Boundaries: Set specific times for social media use rather than checking constantly throughout the day. This prevents unconscious scrolling and helps you engage more intentionally.

Reality Checks: Regularly remind yourself that social media shows limited, curated aspects of people's complete lives. Everyone struggles with things they don't post about.

Emotional Awareness: Notice your emotional state before and after social media sessions. If you consistently feel worse after using certain platforms, consider adjusting your approach.

Take Breaks: Periodically take breaks from social media to reconnect with offline relationships and activities. This helps maintain perspective on the role digital platforms play in your life.

Daily Integration

Today, experiment with using social media more consciously by setting a specific intention before opening any apps. This might be connecting with a particular friend, learning about a topic you're interested in, or sharing something that authentically represents your current experience.

Pay attention to how intentional use feels different from mindless scrolling. Notice when you're engaging authentically versus when you're seeking validation or comparing yourself to others.

Also practice curating your feeds by unfollowing or muting accounts that consistently trigger negative emotions, and engaging more meaningfully with content that supports your well-being and authentic interests.

Tomorrow's Preparation

As you make any financial decisions today—whether spending money, checking account balances, or thinking about financial goals—notice your internal dialogue about money. Pay attention to any anxiety, guilt, or stories you tell yourself about your financial situation. These observations will help us explore conscious money decisions tomorrow.

With this foundation laid within you, you're ready to apply the self-awareness and conscious choice-making you've been developing to your financial life, creating money decisions that align with your authentic values and support your genuine well-being.

Day 27: Money Decisions from Self-Awareness

Before looking at your bank account or thinking about any purchases today, take a moment to notice how you feel about money right now. What emotions come up when you think about your financial situation? Security? Anxiety? Guilt? Excitement? Whatever arises, notice it without trying to change it. Your relationship with money often reflects deeper patterns about self-worth, security, and values.

You probably have a complicated relationship with money that goes far beyond simple budgeting or financial planning. Maybe you feel guilty when you spend money on yourself, or anxious when you can't afford things others seem to buy easily. Perhaps you avoid looking at your financial situation when you're stressed, or you make money decisions based more on emotion than on conscious planning.

Financial decisions offer daily opportunities to practice living from your authentic values rather than unconscious patterns. When you understand how your shadow affects your relationship with money, you can make choices that support both your practical needs and your psychological well-being.

Financial Choices from Wholeness

Most financial advice focuses on strategies and techniques—budgeting methods, investment approaches, debt management systems. But sustainable financial well-being requires understanding the psychological patterns that drive money decisions, many of which operate below conscious awareness.

How Shadow Patterns Affect Money Decisions:

Scarcity Patterns: If you grew up with financial stress or insecurity, parts of you might hoard money even when spending would improve your quality of life, or avoid financial planning because it triggers anxiety.

Worthiness Issues: Beliefs about deserving good things can affect everything from salary negotiations to spending on self-care. You might underspend on yourself while overspending on others.

Control Dynamics: Money often represents security and control. Patterns around control can show up as micromanaging expenses, avoiding financial decisions entirely, or using money to control relationships.

Identity Conflicts: Your spending might reflect who you think you should be rather than who you actually are. You might spend money trying to maintain an image that doesn't align with your authentic values.

Emotional Regulation: Money decisions can be used to manage emotions—spending when sad, hoarding when anxious, or avoiding money entirely when overwhelmed.

Exercise: Values-Based Money Decisions

This exercise helps you identify your authentic financial values and develop decision-making approaches that align with your whole self rather than unconscious patterns.

Step 1: Financial Values Clarification

Explore what you actually value about money, separate from what you think you should value:

Financial Values Exploration:

- What does financial security mean to you personally?

- How important is having expensive things versus having financial flexibility?

- What role do you want money to play in your relationships?

- How do you want to balance saving for the future with enjoying the present?

- What financial achievements would feel genuinely meaningful to you?

- How do you want your money use to reflect your personal values?

Which financial values feel most authentic to who you are rather than what you think you should prioritize?

How do these values compare to the financial messages you received growing up?

Step 2: Shadow Pattern Recognition

Identify unconscious patterns that might interfere with values-based financial decisions:

Common Financial Shadow Patterns:

- Spending money to avoid feeling emotions

- Avoiding financial planning because it triggers anxiety

- Making money decisions based on what others will think

- Using money to control or please others

- Feeling guilty about spending money on yourself

- Avoiding looking at account balances when stressed

Which patterns do you recognize in your own financial behavior?

How might these patterns both protect and limit you financially?

Step 3: Conscious Decision-Making Framework

Develop a process for making financial decisions that integrates both practical considerations and authentic values:

Before Major Financial Decisions, Ask Yourself:

- Does this align with my authentic financial values?

- Am I making this decision from conscious choice or unconscious pattern?

- How will this affect my overall well-being, not just my bank account?

- What am I hoping this purchase or decision will provide for me?

- Could I meet that need in a different way that better aligns with my values?

How might this framework help you make more conscious money decisions?

Step 4: Financial Well-Being Planning

Create specific strategies for using money in ways that support your authentic values and psychological well-being:

- How could you spend more consciously on things that genuinely improve your life?

- What financial boundaries would protect your well-being and values?

- How could you approach financial planning in a way that reduces rather than increases anxiety?

- What support systems would help you maintain conscious financial choices?

What would financial well-being look like for you beyond just having more money?

Reflection Questions

How do your current financial decisions reflect your authentic values versus unconscious patterns?

What would change about your relationship with money if you fully believed you deserved financial well-being?

How might conscious money decisions support your overall shadow integration work?

What role do you want money to play in creating the life you actually want to live?

Creating Financial Security

Financial security means different things to different people, and creating it requires understanding what security actually means to you personally rather than following generic financial advice that might not fit your values or circumstances.

Approaches to Authentic Financial Security:

Align Spending with Values: Instead of just tracking where money goes, actively direct money toward things that support your authentic priorities and well-being.

Plan from Self-Knowledge: Create financial goals based on what you actually want from life rather than what you think you should want or what others expect.

Address Emotional Patterns: Work with the psychological aspects of money management, not just the technical strategies. Your financial behavior is often more about emotions than mathematics.

Build Flexible Security: Create financial stability that can adapt to changing circumstances rather than rigid plans that require perfect conditions.

Integrate Short and Long-term: Balance enjoying life now with preparing for the future in ways that honor both present and future versions of yourself.

Working with Money Anxiety

Financial anxiety is common and often has roots that go deeper than current financial circumstances. Working with this anxiety compassionately can improve both your financial decision-making and your overall quality of life.

Strategies for Money Anxiety:

- Separate realistic financial concerns from anxiety about uncontrollable future scenarios

- Practice looking at your financial situation with curiosity rather than judgment

- Make one small financial improvement at a time rather than trying to fix everything at once

- Connect with others who have healthy relationships with money for perspective and support

- Remember that your worth as a person isn't determined by your financial situation

Daily Integration

Today, make one financial decision consciously by pausing before spending money and asking yourself whether this purchase aligns with your authentic values. This might be as simple as choosing to spend money on something that genuinely improves your well-being rather than something that just fills time or manages emotions.

Pay attention to your internal dialogue about money throughout the day. Notice when you encourage yourself versus when you criticize yourself about financial choices, and practice treating yourself with the same kindness you'd show a friend making similar decisions.

Tomorrow's Preparation

As you think about your future today—next month, next year, the next decade—notice what excites you versus what creates anxiety. Pay attention to whether you're planning from authentic desires or from inherited expectations about what your life should look like. These observations will help us explore conscious future planning tomorrow.

This groundwork opens several pathways to explore how the self-awareness you've been developing can guide major life decisions and long-term planning in ways that honor your authentic self rather than unconscious patterns.

Day 28: Future Planning with Shadow Wisdom

Daily Check-In

Take a moment to imagine yourself five years from now, living in alignment with your authentic values and integrated shadow aspects. What does that version of you look like? How do they spend their time? What kind of relationships do they have? What has changed from who you are today, and what has remained constant? Notice whether this future vision feels exciting and authentic or pressured and performative.

You probably have some vision of where you'd like your life to be heading, but that vision might be influenced more by external expectations than your authentic desires. Maybe you feel pressure to achieve certain milestones by particular ages, or you find yourself planning a future that sounds impressive but doesn't actually excite you when you're honest with yourself.

Shadow-informed future planning means using your growing self-awareness to make long-term decisions based on who you're becoming rather than who you think you should become. This approach creates futures that feel sustainable and fulfilling because they're built on authentic self-knowledge rather than inherited programming.

Long-term Planning with Self-Knowledge

Traditional goal-setting often focuses on external achievements—career progression, financial milestones, lifestyle acquisitions—without much attention to whether these goals align with your authentic values and natural patterns. Shadow-informed planning starts with understanding yourself deeply and then creates external goals that serve your genuine development and well-being.

Elements of Shadow-Informed Future Planning:

Values Integration: Future plans align with your authentic values rather than values you inherited from family, culture, or peer groups. You plan from what actually matters to you, not what you think should matter.

Pattern Awareness: Understanding your natural rhythms, energy patterns, and psychological needs helps create sustainable long-term plans rather than goals that fight against your authentic nature.

Shadow Integration: Plans account for your complete personality, including aspects you've been suppressing. This creates more realistic and fulfilling futures because they're built on your whole self.

Flexible Structure: Plans provide direction while remaining adaptable to growth, changing circumstances, and new discoveries about yourself. Rigid planning often breaks under the pressure of real life.

Process Orientation: Focus on the kind of person you want to become and how you want to live, not just what you want to achieve. This creates sustainable satisfaction because it's based on ongoing experience rather than one-time accomplishments.

Breaking Generational Patterns

Your generation faces unique challenges in future planning because many traditional life paths are no longer reliable or available. This creates opportunities to design life patterns that work better for current conditions, but it also requires letting go of inherited assumptions about how life is supposed to unfold.

Generational Patterns to Examine:

Timeline Expectations: Previous generations often followed predictable sequences—college, career establishment, marriage, home ownership, children, retirement. These timelines might not match your actual opportunities or desires.

Success Definitions: Inherited definitions of success might emphasize external achievements (salary levels, job titles, material possessions) over internal fulfillment (meaningful work, authentic relationships, personal growth).

Security Assumptions: Traditional approaches to security (company loyalty, home ownership, traditional retirement planning) might not work in current economic conditions, requiring new approaches to creating stability.

Relationship Models: Family patterns around partnership, parenting, and social connection might not fit your values or circumstances, requiring conscious creation of new relationship approaches.

Exercise: Future Visioning

This exercise helps you create a future vision based on your authentic self-knowledge and integrated shadow aspects rather than external expectations or unconscious patterns.

Step 1: Authentic Future Visioning

Spend 15-20 minutes in guided visualization, imagining your life 5-10 years from now if you continue integrating your shadow work and living authentically:

Visioning Questions:

- How do you spend your typical day?

- What kind of work are you doing, and how does it align with your values?

- What do your relationships look like, and how do you show up in them?

- How do you handle stress, conflict, and challenges?

- What brings you joy and fulfillment on a regular basis?

- How have you grown from who you are today?

What elements of this future vision feel most exciting and authentic to you?

How does this vision compare to what you thought you "should" want for your future?

Step 2: Integration Gap Analysis

Compare your authentic future vision with your current reality to identify areas for conscious development:

Gap Assessment:

- What aspects of your current life already align with your authentic future vision?

- What would need to change for you to move toward this vision?

- Which changes feel realistic and exciting versus overwhelming or forced?

- What shadow patterns might interfere with creating this authentic future?

- What support, resources, or development would help you move toward this vision?

Which aspects of your future vision feel most achievable and which feel most challenging?

How might your shadow work support movement toward this authentic future?

Step 3: Conscious Goal Setting

Based on your future vision, create specific goals that serve your authentic development:

Shadow-Informed Goals Include:

- Professional development that aligns with your natural strengths and interests

- Relationship goals that support mutual growth and authentic connection

- Financial objectives that reflect your actual values rather than social expectations

- Personal development that integrates your whole self rather than just improving "acceptable" qualities

- Creative or contribution goals that express your authentic gifts and values

Which goals feel most aligned with your authentic self versus which feel driven by external expectations?

Step 4: Implementation Planning

Create realistic strategies for moving toward your authentic future vision:

- What would be meaningful first steps toward each major goal?

- How could you structure your current life to support authentic future development?

- What habits, relationships, or commitments would need to change to align with your vision?

- How will you maintain connection to your authentic vision when external pressures arise?

What implementation strategies feel sustainable and exciting rather than overwhelming or forced?

Reflection Questions

How has your vision of your ideal future changed through shadow work and self-awareness development?

What generational expectations about life success do you need to release to pursue your authentic future?

How might planning from shadow awareness create more fulfilling outcomes than planning from external expectations?

What would you pursue if you fully trusted that your authentic path would lead to fulfillment and contribution?

Conscious Life Design

Conscious life design means creating a lifestyle and life structure that supports your authentic self-expression and continued growth rather than just achieving external markers of success. This approach recognizes that how you live day-to-day is as important as what you achieve.

Principles of Conscious Life Design:

Sustainable Rhythms: Create daily and weekly patterns that work with your natural energy cycles rather than fighting against them. This might mean unconventional schedules that support your authentic productivity and well-being.

Values Integration: Make life choices that consistently express your authentic values rather than compartmentalizing values for certain situations while compromising them in others.

Growth Orientation: Design life experiences that challenge you to develop in directions that feel meaningful rather than just accumulating achievements or maintaining comfort.

Relationship Intention: Consciously cultivate relationships that support mutual authenticity and growth rather than just maintaining social connections that no longer serve you.

Contribution Focus: Include ways to contribute meaningfully to others or causes you care about, recognizing that fulfillment often comes through service as well as personal achievement.

Working with Future Anxiety

Planning for an uncertain future while dealing with global challenges can create anxiety that interferes with conscious decision-making. Working with this anxiety skillfully helps you plan from wisdom rather than fear.

Strategies for Future Anxiety:

- Focus on creating internal resources (skills, relationships, self-awareness) that will serve you regardless of external circumstances

- Balance future planning with present-moment appreciation and engagement

- Accept that some uncertainty is unavoidable and build flexibility into your plans rather than trying to control all outcomes

- Connect with others who are also creating conscious, values-based futures for mutual support and inspiration

- Remember that authentic living is often more resilient than conventional approaches because it's based on your actual strengths and resources

Daily Integration

Today, make one decision based on your authentic future vision rather than immediate convenience or external expectations. This might involve saying no to something that doesn't align with where you want to be heading, or saying yes to an opportunity that serves your long-term authentic development.

Pay attention to how future-focused decisions feel when they're based on self-awareness versus when they're driven by anxiety or social pressure. Notice whether authentic future planning creates excitement or stress.

Tomorrow's Preparation

As you navigate decisions throughout today, notice moments when you check in with your internal wisdom versus when you look primarily to external sources for guidance. Pay attention to how your shadow work has affected your relationship with your own judgment and intuition. These observations will help us explore using your integrated self as a life compass tomorrow.

Having mapped this terrain, you're ready to explore how all the self-awareness you've developed can serve as internal guidance for major life decisions and ongoing navigation of authentic living.

Day 29: Your Shadow as Life Compass

Daily Check-In

Before making any significant decisions today, pause and notice where you typically look for guidance. Do you immediately consult others, research expert opinions, or worry about making the "right" choice? Or do you have a sense of your own inner wisdom and trust your ability to navigate from authentic self-knowledge? Both approaches have value, but many people have lost connection to their internal compass.

You've probably experienced moments when you knew something was right or wrong for you before you could explain why rationally. Maybe you felt immediately comfortable with someone you just met, or uneasy about an opportunity that looked perfect on paper. This internal guidance system often knows things your conscious mind hasn't figured out yet, but it requires trust and attention to access.

Your integrated shadow—the parts of yourself you've learned to recognize and work with consciously—can serve as a sophisticated guidance system for life decisions. Instead of seeing shadow aspects as problems to solve, you can learn to read them as information about what serves your authentic development and what works against it.

Using Shadow for Direction

Your shadow patterns often activate more strongly when you're moving away from authentic alignment and settle down when you're moving toward choices that serve your whole self. This makes them valuable early warning systems and confirmation signals for life decisions.

How Shadow Patterns Provide Guidance:

Energy Changes: Notice when situations consistently energize you versus drain you. Your authentic path usually feels sustainable and engaging rather than forcing you to override your natural rhythms constantly.

Reaction Intensities: Strong emotional reactions often point toward important values or needs that are being honored or violated. Pay attention to what triggers intense responses and what that might reveal about your authentic priorities.

Pattern Activation: When familiar shadow patterns become more prominent, it often means you're in situations that don't support your integrated self. When shadow patterns feel less compelling, you're likely in better alignment.

Physical Sensations: Your body often knows before your mind whether something is right for you. Notice tension, relaxation, excitement, or discomfort as information about authentic alignment.

Creative Flow: When you're in alignment with your authentic path, creative and innovative thinking often flows more easily. When you're forcing yourself into misaligned situations, creativity typically diminishes.

One person described using their shadow as guidance: "I noticed that my people-pleasing patterns always got worse when I was in jobs that didn't fit my values. When I started paying attention to that, I could tell pretty quickly whether a work environment would support my authentic self or trigger my old patterns of trying to be who others needed me to be."

Exercise: Shadow-Informed Choices

This exercise teaches you to use your growing shadow awareness as guidance for making decisions that support your authentic development and well-being.

Step 1: Current Decision Assessment

237

Choose a decision you're currently facing—it might be professional, personal, relational, or lifestyle-related. This exercise works best with decisions where you're genuinely uncertain about the best choice.

Decision Context:

- What decision are you trying to make?

- What options are you considering?

- What external advice or information have you gathered?

- What practical considerations are affecting this decision?

- Why does this decision feel important or challenging to you?

What makes this decision feel significant for your life direction?

Step 2: Shadow Pattern Consultation

Examine how each option in your decision might affect your shadow patterns and overall authenticity:

For Each Option, Consider:

- How would this choice affect your energy levels and overall well-being?

- Which shadow patterns might this option trigger or strengthen?

- Which aspects of your authentic self would this choice support or suppress?

- How does your body respond when you imagine choosing this option?

- What concerns or excitements arise when you consider this choice?

Which option feels most aligned with your integrated self rather than just your "acceptable" persona?

What is your shadow awareness telling you about each choice?

Step 3: Values and Integration Check

Assess how each option aligns with your authentic values and supports continued shadow integration:

Integration Assessment Questions:

- Which choice would allow you to express more of your whole self?

- How would each option support or interfere with your ongoing personal growth?

- Which choice feels sustainable for your natural rhythms and needs?

- What would each option require you to suppress or emphasize about yourself?

- How does each choice connect to your authentic future vision?

Which option most supports your continued authenticity and integration?

Step 4: Decision Integration Planning

Based on your shadow-informed assessment, make your choice and plan how to implement it consciously:

- What does your internal guidance suggest about this decision?

- How will you maintain awareness of shadow patterns as you implement this choice?

- What support or resources will help you stay authentic while making this change?

- How will you adjust if your choice needs modification based on new information?

How does making decisions from shadow awareness feel different from other decision-making approaches you've used?

Reflection Questions

How has your relationship with your own judgment and internal wisdom changed through shadow work?

What would change about your life decisions if you fully trusted your integrated self as a guidance system?

How do you distinguish between authentic internal guidance and anxiety, wishful thinking, or old patterns?

What role do you want internal wisdom to play alongside external information in your decision-making?

Trusting Inner Wisdom

Learning to trust your internal guidance system requires distinguishing between authentic wisdom and the various forms of internal noise—anxiety, wishful thinking, old programming, or reactive emotions. This discernment develops through practice and attention to how different internal experiences feel and what results they create.

Characteristics of Authentic Internal Guidance:

Calm Clarity: Authentic guidance usually feels calm and clear rather than urgent or emotionally charged. It often comes through quiet knowing rather than dramatic insights.

Sustainable Direction: Internal wisdom typically points toward choices that feel sustainable long-term rather than exciting in the moment but exhausting to maintain.

Values Alignment: Authentic guidance aligns with your genuine values and supports your continued growth and authenticity.

Wholeness Integration: True internal wisdom includes both practical considerations and authentic self-expression rather than sacrificing one for the other.

Flexible Certainty: Authentic guidance feels solid without being rigid—confident about direction while remaining open to course corrections based on new information.

Major Life Decision-Making

For significant life decisions—career changes, relationship commitments, geographic moves, major financial choices—using shadow awareness as guidance can provide valuable information that purely rational analysis might miss.

Process for Shadow-Informed Major Decisions:

1. **Gather Information**: Research practical considerations and external perspectives while remaining open to internal wisdom.

2. **Create Space**: Give yourself time for reflection without pressure to decide immediately. Major decisions often require both analysis and integration time.

3. **Notice Patterns**: Pay attention to which options consistently energize you versus drain you over time, not just initial excitement.

4. **Consult Your Body**: Use physical sensations as information—tension, relaxation, excitement, dread—about different choices.

5. **Check Integration**: Assess which options support your continued authenticity and shadow integration rather than requiring you to suppress important aspects of yourself.

6. **Plan Consciously**: Once you choose, plan implementation in ways that support your authentic self rather than forcing adaptation to external requirements.

Working with Decision Anxiety

Using internal guidance for important decisions can trigger anxiety, especially if you're used to relying primarily on external validation or expert advice. This anxiety often reflects fears about trusting yourself rather than concerns about specific decisions.

Common Decision-Making Fears:

- Worry about making the "wrong" choice and facing consequences

- Anxiety about trusting yourself when others might disagree

- Fear that internal guidance isn't practical or realistic

- Concern about being selfish by prioritizing authentic preferences

- Worry about changing your mind or needing to adjust decisions later

Working with Decision Anxiety Skillfully:

- Remember that most decisions can be adjusted if circumstances change or you learn new information

- Accept that some uncertainty is normal when making choices about unknown futures

- Balance internal guidance with practical considerations rather than seeing them as conflicting approaches

- Connect with others who support your authentic development rather than only people who want you to make conventional choices

- Practice self-compassion about the complexity of major life decisions

Daily Integration

Today, use your shadow awareness as guidance for at least one decision, even if it's relatively small. Pay attention to how different choices feel in your body and what your energy patterns tell you about various options.

Notice the difference between decisions made from authentic internal guidance and those made primarily from anxiety, social pressure, or overthinking. Practice trusting your internal wisdom while also gathering appropriate external information.

Tomorrow's Preparation

Tonight, take some time to appreciate the growth and self-awareness you've developed over these 29 days of shadow work. Tomorrow is your graduation day, and you'll be integrating everything you've learned into plans for continuing this work independently. Reflect on how your relationship with yourself has changed and what aspects of this work you want to maintain going forward.

Armed with this understanding, you're ready to celebrate your shadow work journey and create sustainable practices for continuing this important psychological and spiritual development throughout your life.

Day 30: Your Ongoing Shadow Work Journey

Daily Check-In

Take a moment to appreciate yourself for completing this 30-day journey of shadow work. You've examined parts of yourself that most people spend their entire lives avoiding. You've developed skills for working consciously with unconscious patterns. You've practiced authentic expression in relationships, work, and creative activities. This represents a significant accomplishment in personal growth and self-awareness.

As you prepare to graduate from this structured program, notice any feelings that arise. Relief at finishing? Sadness about the program ending? Excitement about applying what you've learned? Anxiety about maintaining the work without daily guidance? All of these reactions are normal and provide information about how you want to continue your shadow work journey.

Graduation doesn't mean you've completed shadow work—it means you've developed tools and awareness that will continue evolving throughout your life. Today is about celebrating your growth while creating sustainable practices for ongoing integration and authentic living.

Celebrating Transformation

Before thinking about future practices, take time to acknowledge the specific changes you've experienced through this process. Transformation often happens gradually, and it's easy to minimize growth or take new awareness for granted.

Areas of Potential Growth Over 30 Days:

Self-Awareness: You likely have much clearer understanding of your patterns, triggers, values, and authentic preferences. This awareness creates foundation for more conscious choices.

Relationship Skills: You may find yourself communicating more directly, setting boundaries more easily, and recognizing projection patterns in conflicts with others.

Professional Authenticity: You might be bringing more of your genuine self to work situations, making career decisions based on authentic values, or recognizing when work environments don't support your whole self.

Creative Expression: You may have reconnected with creative activities, found new outlets for authentic self-expression, or integrated creativity into daily life more regularly.

Internal Dialogue: Your relationship with different aspects of yourself has likely become more compassionate and curious rather than critical and controlling.

Decision-Making: You probably have better access to internal wisdom and clearer sense of what choices support your authentic development.

One person reflected on their transformation: "I didn't realize how much energy I was spending trying to be who I thought others needed me to be. Now I have so much more energy because I'm not constantly managing my image or suppressing parts of myself. I feel more like myself than I have in years."

Maintaining Practice

The key to sustaining shadow work benefits is developing practices that realistically fit into your actual lifestyle rather than idealized versions of what consistent self-improvement should look like.

Sustainable Shadow Work Practices:

Weekly Check-ins: Schedule brief weekly time for reflection on patterns, triggers, and authentic choices. This maintains awareness without requiring daily intensive practice.

Integration Journaling: Write periodically about how shadow work insights apply to current life situations. This helps transfer awareness into practical application.

Creative Expression: Maintain some form of creative activity that allows unconscious material to emerge and provides outlet for authentic self-expression.

Conscious Communication: Continue practicing direct, honest communication in relationships while taking responsibility for your own emotional reactions and projections.

Values-Based Decision Making: Use your growing self-awareness as guidance for major and minor life choices, checking decisions against authentic values rather than external expectations.

Creating Support Systems

Shadow work is easier to maintain when you have support from others who understand and encourage this kind of psychological development. Building community around growth helps normalize the ongoing process of becoming more authentic.

Types of Support for Ongoing Shadow Work:

Growth-Oriented Relationships: Cultivate friendships and romantic partnerships with people who appreciate your authenticity and support your continued development rather than preferring you to stay the same.

Professional Support: Consider working with therapists, coaches, or other professionals who understand shadow work and can provide guidance when patterns feel stuck or overwhelming.

Learning Communities: Join book clubs, workshops, online forums, or other communities focused on personal growth, psychology, or spiritual development that resonates with your approach.

Mentorship: Find mentors who demonstrate the kind of integrated, authentic living you want to develop, and consider becoming a mentor to others who are beginning their own growth journey.

Creative Community: Connect with others around creative activities that support authentic self-expression and provide outlets for ongoing integration work.

Resource Guide for Continued Growth

Books for Continued Shadow Work:

- Books on Jungian psychology and shadow work principles

- Memoirs by people who demonstrate authentic, integrated living

- Books on creativity, relationships, and career authenticity

- Resources specific to challenges you want to continue working with

Professional Resources:

- Therapists trained in depth psychology, Jungian analysis, or Internal Family Systems

- Coaches who specialize in authentic living and values-based decision making

- Spiritual directors or guides if religious/spiritual integration appeals to you

Online Resources:

- Podcasts about psychology, personal growth, and authentic living

- Online courses in areas where you want continued development

- Social media accounts that provide ongoing inspiration and practical guidance

Experiential Resources:

- Workshops on topics like communication skills, creative expression, or leadership development

- Retreat experiences that provide time for deeper self-reflection and integration

- Travel or other experiences that challenge you to grow in authentic directions

Working with Integration Challenges

As you continue shadow work independently, you'll encounter periods when old patterns feel more prominent or when integration feels difficult. These challenges are normal parts of the growth process rather than signs of failure.

Common Ongoing Challenges:

Pattern Regression: During stress or major life changes, old shadow patterns often resurface. This provides opportunities for deeper integration rather than evidence that you haven't grown.

Relationship Adjustments: As you become more authentic, some relationships may change or end while others deepen. This can be emotionally challenging but often leads to more satisfying connections.

External Pressure: Family, work, or social environments might resist your increased authenticity and encourage you to return to familiar patterns. Maintaining growth requires ongoing commitment to your authentic development.

Integration Overwhelm: Sometimes the complexity of continued growth can feel overwhelming. It's important to work at sustainable paces and seek support when needed.

Purpose Evolution: As you integrate shadow aspects, your sense of purpose and direction may shift. This can be exciting but also disorienting as you navigate new possibilities.

Your Ongoing Journey

Shadow work is lifelong process rather than project with completion point. Each life stage brings new opportunities for integration and authentic expression as circumstances change and you continue developing.

Ongoing Journey Principles:

Patience with Process: Growth happens gradually through consistent small choices rather than dramatic transformations. Trust that integration continues even when progress isn't obvious.

Self-Compassion During Setbacks: Treat yourself with kindness when old patterns resurface or when growth feels difficult. Self-criticism usually slows integration rather than accelerating it.

Curiosity About Changes: Remain open to discovering new aspects of yourself and to changing directions when authentic development leads in unexpected ways.

Service Integration: Look for ways to use your growing authenticity and self-awareness to contribute meaningfully to others or causes you care about.

Joy in Authenticity: Remember that the goal isn't perfect integration but increased capacity for authentic living, creative expression, and genuine connection with others.

Daily Integration

Today, create a simple plan for maintaining shadow work practices that feels realistic for your lifestyle. This might include weekly reflection time, monthly creative expression, regular check-ins with supportive friends, or professional support when needed.

Also spend time appreciating specific growth you've experienced through this process. Write about or share with others how your relationship with yourself and your life has changed through shadow work.

Finally, set intentions for how you want to continue growing and what aspects of authentic living you most want to develop over the coming months and years.

Completion and New Beginning

Congratulations on completing this 30-day shadow work journey. You've developed tools and awareness that will serve your authentic development for the rest of your life. The structured program ends today, but your relationship with your whole self—including shadow aspects—will continue evolving and deepening.

Remember that this work is never finished, and that's what makes it interesting. Each day offers new opportunities to choose authenticity over performance, consciousness over automatic patterns, and integration over compartmentalization. You have everything you need to continue this important work of becoming more yourself while contributing meaningfully to the world around you.

Trust yourself, be patient with your process, and remember that your authentic presence is a gift to others who are also learning to live more truthfully. Your shadow work creates permission for others to embrace their own complexity and wholeness.

"The work of integration continues, but now you have the tools and awareness to navigate it consciously."

Now that you've explored this territory, you're prepared for a lifetime of authentic living, conscious choice-making, and ongoing integration of your complete self in service of both personal fulfillment and meaningful contribution to the world.

References

1. Al-Khouja, M., et al. (2022). "Self-expression can be authentic or inauthentic, with differential outcomes for well-being." *Journal of Research in Personality*. Links authenticity to positive mental health outcomes.

2. Bailey, E. R., et al. (2020). "Authentic self-expression on social media is associated with greater subjective well-being." *Nature Communications*, 11, 4889. Shows authentic expression correlates with life satisfaction.

3. Boivin, D. B., et al. (2021). "Disturbance of the Circadian System in Shift Work and Its Health Impact." *PMC8832572*. Reviews scientific evidence on circadian disruption effects.

4. Campbell, J. (Ed.). (1976). *The Portable Jung*. Penguin Classics. Accessible compilation of Jung's core concepts on shadow integration.

5. Cooper, M., & Knox, R. (2018). "Self-expression and psychological well-being in counselling practice." *Counselling Directory*. Links authentic expression to healthy relationships and boundary setting.

6. Deloitte Global. (2024). *Gen Z and Millennial Survey 2024: Mental Health Deep Dive*. Shows that 40% of Gen Z and 35% of millennials feel stressed or anxious most of the time.

7. Deloitte. (2024). "Meeting The Needs And Expectations Of Gen Zs and Millennials on Workplace Mental Health." *Forbes*. 50% of Gen Z and millennials report workplace burnout.

8. Hancock, J., et al. (2022). "Psychological Well-Being and Social Media Use: A Meta-Analysis." *Social Science*

Research Network. Meta-analysis of 226 studies showing social media's impact on mental health.

9. Harvard Health Publishing. (2023). "Shift work can harm sleep and health: What helps?" Links non-standard schedules to metabolic syndrome and mental health issues.

10. Ipsos. (2024). *World Mental Health Day Report 2024*. Global statistics on mental health challenges, particularly affecting younger demographics.

11. Jeffrey, S. (2023). "A Beginner's Guide to Jungian Shadow Work." *Scott Jeffrey Insights*. Comprehensive guide to shadow work principles and practices.

12. Johnson, R. A. (1989). *Inner Work: Using Dreams and Active Imagination for Personal Growth*. HarperOne. Practical applications of Jungian shadow work.

13. Jung, C. G. (1945). "The Philosophical Tree." In *Alchemical Studies: The Collected Works of C.G. Jung, Volume 13*. Princeton University Press. Contains the famous quote about making the unconscious conscious.

14. Jung, C. G. (1968). *Man and His Symbols*. Dell Publishing. Original foundational work on shadow psychology and individuation.

15. Jung, C. G. (1972). *Two Essays on Analytical Psychology: The Collected Works of C.G. Jung, Volume 7*. Princeton University Press. Defines individuation and personality integration.

16. McLaughlin, R. G. (2014). "Shadow Work in Support of the Adult Developmental Journey." *Digital Commons at Lesley University*. Qualitative study on shadow work's role in adult development.

17. Mul Fedele, M., et al. (2024). "Bridging the gap: examining circadian biology and fatigue in shift workers." *Nature*

Scientific Reports. Analyzes different work schedules' impacts on worker well-being.

18. Naslund, J. A., et al. (2020). "Social Media and Mental Health: Benefits, Risks, and Opportunities for Research and Practice." *Journal of Medical Internet Research*, 22(4). PMC7785056.

19. Night Owls vs Early Birds Research. (2025). "How Procrastination and Sleep Patterns Connect." *Ahead App.* Shows 40% of productivity tendencies attributed to chronotype alignment.

20. Ostic, D., et al. (2021). "Effects of Social Media Use on Psychological Well-Being." *PMC8255677*. Shows both positive and negative effects coexist in social media use.

21. Plackett, R., et al. (2023). "The Impact of Social Media Use Interventions on Mental Well-Being." *Journal of Medical Internet Research*, 25. Shows therapy-based interventions more effective than abstinence.

22. QR Code Generator. (2025). *Gen Z and Millennials Drive Surge in NHS Mental Health Service Use*. Psychreg.org. Documents 35% increase in millennial mental health service use over three years.

23. Randler, C., et al. (2006). "Morningness-eveningness compared to extraversion, conscientiousness, mental toughness, and self-regulation." *Personality and Individual Differences*. Links personality traits to chronotype preferences.

24. Roberts, A. (2021). "Writing-As-Shadow-Work: An Aesthetics of Jungian Psychoanalysis." *University of Salford Repository*. Explores creative expression as shadow integration tool.

25. Roenneberg, T., et al. (2007). "The human circadian clock entrains to sun time." *Current Biology*. Foundational research on individual chronotype differences.

26. Rogers, C. R. (1957). "The necessary and sufficient conditions of therapeutic personality change." *Journal of Consulting Psychology*. Foundational work on authentic self-expression in relationships.

27. Sedikides, C., & Schlegel, R. J. (2024). "Distilling the concept of authenticity." *Nature Reviews Psychology*. Comprehensive review of authenticity research and psychological functioning.

28. Silva, I., et al. (2023). "Consequences of Shift Work and Night Work: A Literature Review." *PMC10218650*. Documents psychological impacts of misaligned schedules on well-being.

29. Society of Analytical Psychology. (2023). "The Jungian Shadow." Official resource on shadow psychology from certified Jungian analysts.

30. Stirland, L. E., et al. (2023). "Authenticity and brain health: a values-based perspective." *PMC10432154*. Connects authentic living to neurological well-being.

31. UCLA Health. (2024). "5 long-term health effects of shift work." Documents cancer, cardiovascular disease, and mental health impacts.

32. Valkenburg, P. M., et al. (2022). "Social media use and well-being: What we know and what we need to know." *Current Opinion in Psychology*. Comprehensive review of social media's psychological impacts.

33. World Health Organization & International Labour Organization. (2021). "WHO/ILO Joint Estimates of the Work-related Burden of Disease and Injury, 2000–2016." Shows 745,000 deaths from overwork-related health issues.

34. Wu, Q-J., et al. (2022). "Shift work and health outcomes: an umbrella review of systematic reviews and meta-analyses." *Journal of Clinical Sleep Medicine*, 18(2):653–662.

www.ingramcontent.com/pod-product-compliance
Lightning Source LLC
Chambersburg PA
CBHW072119270326
41931CB00010B/1609